p. 55

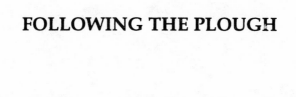

FOLLOWING THE PLOUGH

FOLLOWING THE PLOUGH

RECOVERING THE RURAL

SELECTED AND EDITED BY

JOHN B. LEE

BLACK MOSS PRESS

2000

Published by Black Moss Press, 2450 Byng Road, Windsor, Ontario N8W 3E8, Canada. Black Moss books are distributed in Canada and the U.S. by Firefly Books.

Black Moss Press would like to acknowledge the generous support of the Canada Council for the Arts as well as the Ontario Arts Council for its publishing program this year.

Canadian Cataloguing In Publication Data

Lee, John B., 1951 —
  Following The Plough

ISBN 0-88753-338-8

  1. Title

PR8573.E348F58 2000   C811'.54 C00-900565-X
PR9199.3.L39F64 2000

CONTENTS

FOREWORD

FOLLOWING THE PLOUGH
RECOVERING THE RURAL

Now the plough follows the farmer, where once a plowman followed the furrow in the wake of his horse-drawn plough. My own grandfather walked the seam of turning earth and saw the sweating team and felt the pull and rock of difficult work, holding handles down and wrapped by leather lines to his waist as he claimed the land. His son, my father, came to ride the fuming horse of another age, while there behind his share curved like a human hip the plough blade cut the earth as it rolled away behind him. And now, a stranger works that land.

And so, not to make too much of the metaphor, we writers follow the furrow of those who have gone before. From Piers plowman through poet and ploughman's son, John Clare with the enclosure of late eighteenth century Northamptonshire, England to our very own poet farmer, Raymond Knister, we live in a long line of those who came before us. The world is changing and ever more human. However, the one eternal truth is that the land will survive us. And poets celebrate the connection between themselves and the earth. Whether they are remembering the farm as it was, or seeing what has become of it with much neglect, or perhaps they are seeing how the land is changed by the very act of cultivation, or they are looking with longing at a disappearing world made over-human by our presence, still they see the land in language and make a way for others to follow.

Raymond Knister's poem, "The Plowman," seems an apt beginning:

All day I follow
Watching the swift dark furrow
That curls away before me,
And care not for skies or upturned flowers,
And at the end of the field
Look backward
Ever with discontent.
A stone, a root, a strayed thought

Has warped the line of that furrow —
And urge my horses 'round again.
Sometimes even before the row is finished
I must look backward;
To find, when I come to the end
That there I swerved.

Unappeased I leave the field,
Expectant, return.

The horses are very patient.
When I tell myself
This time
The ultimate unflawed turning
Is before my share,
They must give up their rest.

This book is dedicated to that first great modern Canadian poet, Raymond Knister, who wrote about the land with a clean, clear, uncluttered style. His poem, "The Plowman" in an early draft ended with these lines:

Some day, some day, be sure
I shall turn the furrow of all my hopes.
But I shall not, doing it, look backward.

Yet we do look back, look forward, regard the world around us, and seek a way to say the way we see — the land, nature, agriculture, the village within, the animal kingdom, the peaceable garden — we remember, we dream, we long, we live and are connected...

— John B. Lee

BEFORE WE GAVE THEM NAMES

George Swede

I should know what to call
that bird whose song
makes my breath slow
and that sky-sweeping tree
from which the bird sings
I should know what to call
these common wild flowers
aglow with their yellowness
in the evening light
I'm supposed to be
a lover of nature
yes, but at this moment
I'm a lover of things
the way they were
before we gave them names

FEEDING THE POWER GRID

Bert Almon

As we drove through the Battle River valley
he gave us a social history of the farms
on the east side of the road: who had died
childless; whose children moved to town
and sold the land to strangers; who is banned
from owning any cattle after the winter
twenty of them stood starving inside
a fancy electrified fence. Once in a while
the stories are racy: "That guy married a big woman
with hair on her face who could whip
a grizzly bear with a switch." He doesn't look once
to the west, where great mounds of fresh clay

have been tossed up by the drag lines. The strip mine
will pursue the coal a hundred meters down
to feed the power grids of Western Canada.
This was the farm where he and my wife grew up,
the place where their mother's ashes were scattered.
"Dust to dust," "the common clay"-fine phrases,
but the mine goes deeper than gossip or Genesis:
there was no oral history in the Cretaceous.
His past burns like filaments in a light bulb.

BREATHING LILACS

Sylvia Adams

Few flowers attach so many memories.
Few make us grow younger with each quiver.
I'm back in those early June mornings,
bedsheets sailing the backyard line,
spinnakers of shirts heaving
into the blue swell of sky,
the hollow syllable of screen slapping wood,
a frieze of cats - always
outdoor cats those faraway days -
on the porch step, poised
to inhale the robin's throb.
Here is the garden where rhubarb plotted takeover,
where bees grumbled into wakefulness
among morning glories
and breezes harmonized on strings
stretched taut for butter beans to climb;
and down the street at noon, the clop of
the last village horse, unaware
of imminent retirement, trundled the milkman's bottles.
Evenings, a girl with crimped hair and bows
and a boy whose hand covered hers like a bear's paw
leaned into the last bruised light,
whispers lost in victrola strains

from a glowing throat of window.
Who would guess this world would someday seem
a curiosity, something the children call the olden days
that I, breathing lilacs, could evoke and welcome
learning the language all over again

BRIER ISLAND

Janice Kulyk Keefer

In the beginning, this:
white water,
black rock.
Sea dizzy with the swill
and slam of salt.

Our genesis:
semen and amniotic sac,
blood ties—
salt-licking life.
*

Brier Island marks land's end.
Against it ocean smashing
glass.
Cormorants fly,
necks cocked like pistols:
stones pelted, dark to dark.
*

Winter—the lighthouse plays
blindman's bluff with fishing boats.
Ice dissevering
brute rock—no snow but foam
dulling the blade of shore.
One Iron ring, keening
against an iron pole.
*

Spring, and sheep graze

precarious, on barbed grass.
Under the flagpole
strawberries erupt from stone,
minute Andromedas our mouths
unchain.
*
Land's end: base elements
yet incongruities absurd enough
for miracles:

voluptuary iris
spikes through arid basalt,

lovers on a ledge
no wider than an operating table
tipped over the smash of water, rock.

Flesh pounds and breaks
imaginable
zero.

"FAST DRIVES THE SNOW, AND NO MAN COMES THIS WAY." — "IN NOVEMBER" - LAMPMAN

Sylvia Adams

You were born in the same year as Bliss and Tagore,
the year Victoria donned widow's weeds
and the source of the Nile beckoned Burton and Speke;
the first year of Lincoln's presidency;
when Freud was a schoolboy in breeches
and Browning buried his wife of fifteen years.
The world was opening up,
finding room for you.

It was November; winter beginning,
and so little space for you,
enough only for a short life,
an early yearning toward the grave.
It's hard for us to imagine
your dramas playing out
against the gaslight's chiaroscuro
horse-drawn cutters
carving arteries through your winters.
Hard to edit out that soulless mechanization
you feared and we grew up with -
that has encroached and encroaches still.
How many poets since you saw the End of Things -
anthologized World Wars, Wasteland,
a rough beast slouching?

I picture you on that wooded path
wrapping yourself in snow
and insisting you're content to watch and dream.
Maybe you were, as long as spring was coming.

Call forth one more nuthatch,
coax one more adder's tongue out of the earth,

tell me again what solitude is,
what the dark shades say
as the lamps dim on another century

It's still cold here,
and we don't know where we're going

PIONEER POEM

Kemeny Babineau

down come tree

          up go barn

down come tree

          up go house

     out come stump, round go fence
      off come rock, up go wall

             down tree

       out road

             down grain
       off boat

         up more

      down tree

        up house

       hoe crop

        lay road

    fill boat

here come cousin Jack
and "Mary," someone said

     "we cant go back."

16

A TOSS OF CONES

Brian Bartlett

Twelve months, and one more ring to the tree —
a measurement of years, hidden as our marrow.
Show me a table that grows like that.

No alder chair lets leaves go in October
and unfolds others in May. No birch garden-stake
twists to left or right, hungry for sunlight.
A bird's-eye-maple bowl doesn't throw
many-branched shadows over the ground
any more than ashes broadcast on the wind
are a man or woman remembered and mourned.

Don't talk to me about the afterlife of trees.
I need places where sap drops in a bucket
and jack pines start up through fire-blackened soil,

where wingseeds spin down through air, a toss
of cones on the orange earth.

In this world in a minute you can walk — for now,
you can walk — from dim woods where firs squeeze
out other firs, like too many fish feeding in a pool,

to one butternut tree on a riverbank
spreading its limbs like an embrace of the air.

After breathing paper too long, be glad to know
a white elm drinks fifteen hundred gallons of water
from a hot dawn to a hot dusk

and Moroccan goats climb to the highest branches
                                        of argan trees
to eat the sweet leaves and bark.

THE SNOWSCAPE PUZZLE

Marianne Bluger

RIght there at the edge of imagining
is what happens in the end.
You know it as you blench, your heart knocks
and the pieces lock
in the only picture possible.

As when we walked last night
through moonlit fields:
'Winter on the Farm.'

Wherever we moved on the radiant snows
we heard Mare
whinny her longing to draw the sled.
And now the fields in morning light
lie widely bruised with night-blue prints.

Mare shifts to the back of her stall.

She will sleep on her legs — for years perhaps
till a chance blast come, some rushing wind
and the door crash down.

In the meantime you might find this poem
printed in some magazine.

Obsession —
to press the last piece down.

UPPER-CANADIAN OAK

John B. Lee

They say two hundred years ago
the oak were tall enough to touch
above the light
an ancient wisdom in the wood
five hundred summers old
and a two-chain girth
in the long-lost rains
of the past before the past
in the axe and wedge and stump-rot
of arriving Europe
when language of land
was wind-simple
and thrilled with weed.

I will not hearken back
to when wolves
romanced the hills of night
without response
as if the lonely moon
were lonelier for that
primordial ulul’arum of the beast.

But what is lost
by ghosts is lost by all
and to know
the nameless rivers knew their names
in the dream-nation of themselves
where water laughs
to lap the shallow rocks
and suck the surface down
in the foamy lashing
of a phantom sky
which never happens twice
and never happens there
unless the water deepens on its own.

And if by dying well
we are to do some good
as it is with
dying into someone else's memory:
a slow forgetting —
the welter of weather
on a stone transformed
until it is no longer stone
— a making way

a soul looks down
and loves the child
who holds the past within his heart
six-thousand-year-old cities
rise and fall
within the fertile crescent
of an unborn womb
and like a velvet clock
the silken circle
receives the dreaming seed.

NORTH FROM YARMOUTH

James Deahl

This clump of low
        roses
spotted with wild, red hips

offers the only shelter
from the remorseless
        wind.

With nothing
        but the autumn sea

filling my ears

I stand bathed by cold sunlight
watching as seasons
                    change.

The men and women who piled
                    these stones
to keep back the sea

are all dead;
their pastures lie under
                    asters and goldenrod.

Grouse nest
            where barns stood.
I watch long rollers run in

as those others must have done
on rising to reach for
                    that next rock.

STREAM UNDER FLIGHT

John Livingston Clark

your shack's on the edge of a working field, but you don't
work the garden much anymore. a few herbs and onions, a hill
of spuds the rest gone to hell and purple loose-strife. mean-
while — on the highway south — crows feast daily on some poor
creature's fate. is man just a crow with occasional manners?
appetite is appetite: beaks and teeth. yet how quiet you've
become amidst elms and spruce, muttering over a bowl of cold
rice, slumbering with pen and empty paper. maybe there is a
way; the rise and fall of a single breath; the end of a line where
someone blossoms.

if you're looking for a place to rest your mind, forget the Rocks or those western isles. tourists flock there like gulls at a dump, and the clink of silver is louder than hell. why not seek the humblest place—buy a shack and sit still on the edge of a field. on one gets tanned like the coyotes here, no one eats better than the ducks and crows. and all year long birds visit from afar; goldfinches, orioles, meadowlarks, geese. even lofty pelicans on their way up north. after years of handshakes—the honesty of wings.

* * *

the road to your shack is the one ploughs forget, no tire tracks ever rutting the snow. just waxwings and chickadees flitting through the trees—a neighbour's pigeons, some skunks on the ground. everything's closed and the rats in those granaries remember fatter times. but who has better trees? all the yards overgrown with aspen and spruce. folks move on but trees keep the centre. what is there really to chase anymore? at the end of the road abandon your car. each step a breath, each breath a journey.

ABANDONED FARMHOUSES

Brent Robillard

They litter the countryside
like seeds thrown
from a careless hand
sprouting hard and tough
among stones
among stunted apple trees
and fallow fields
on the roads
to Harlem,
Rideau Ferry
and the Burnt Hills
around Kingston.

The wind knows them
by name, keeps
about their boarded windows
a constant vigil
knocks lightly
at their battered doors
and is invited in through cracks
in the slowly decomposing walls
to wander aimlessly up the stairs
and down the hallways
into rooms where farmers laid
their tired bones
in sunken mattresses
and slept and dreamt
the tight-eyed dream
of better seasons
in the days when they still believed
the land would yield
more than rock
more than heartache.

WHY?

Betsy Struthers

Imagine you[1] are in a field in mid-July, reaping wheat
for the third straight day and everything is chaff: stings
your eyes, plugs your nose, coats your dry tongue, itches
every inch of skin both bare and clothed. And in your ears
only the rhythm of the scythe: so hot, so hot, so hot.
Repetitive strain burns stripes along your shoulders,
your palms blister, bleed. All to put bread on the table,
Father at the head, hands folded. What he says is grace.
You fill every mouth except your own.

     No wonder on Saturday nights you drink too much,
lips loose with schemes and silly rhymes your friends applaud.
Their laughter veils your tears. And when you dance, oh!
when you dance: the beat transports you till you fall. That
kind of sleep at least is dreamless.

     There is a crow in your path, hunched over carrion.
Alone you see how light gilds its wings, that gloss on black.

     A small voice in your head rejoicing.

     To listen at last, open your mouth to free it. To
take to the road to bear witness. God, it's unnerving
in the beginning, the words, and the people come
to hear them. You talk of love and they listen, rapt, still.

     I could go along with you for this.

     I could say for you amen.

---

1 Henry Alline, the New Light Prophet to the Maritimes, 1748-1784. Italicized quotations in the poems are from *The Journal of Henry Alline*, ed. James Beverley and Barry Moody (Hantsport, NS: Lancelot Press, 1982.) Footnoted quotes are from the King James Version of the Bible.

ONE RED APPLE
for Jennifer

Mary Hutchman

Thanksgiving family tradition,
my grandparents' farm at the centre
we leave the city behind
to wander the land: sisters and brothers,
mothers, grandmothers, great-aunts
walk down the laneway
toward the sweet smelling
cedar grove, where Ikey,
an Indian from Tyendinega, lived
for thirty years, silent addition
to my mother's family, a squatter
whose heritage resonates still.

I watch my three-year-old niece
in her red cardigan
short legs blue-jeaned,
straight brown hair cut in a bob
encircling her sweet round face,
bangs innocently fringing blue eyes
taking in the wonder of the land.
Bending down, her little hands
cup the bounty of her walk:
in one hand, one red apple,
in the other, a rock.

MRS. TUCKER AND THE BLACKBERRIES

Sue Wheeler

She laughed when I gave her the jam. "Those damn
blackberries! The years I slaved to get rid
of them!" I don't have the heart to tell her
what's gone: the barn on the hill, the slipways
where Clyde Tucker hauled out boats for repair.

Her bluebells run in right angles, cabin
sunk to the sketch someone made by lamplight.
Autumns, the men would hitch to Alberta
for the money in wheat. On her own with
kids, horses, cow, the crops to get in—

those spiky arms waiting to take it back.
Vines fat as a man's thumb will grab your hair,
your sweater, as if they sense you and reach,
each leaf a dark contract: "Do what you must.
We've got all the time in the world."

KEEPING UP APPEARANCES

Derk Wynand

Winter apples dotted trees without leaves,
a mist slowly washing the black branches
and fruit away, as in Chinese landscapes,
hints of more solid mountains here and there
in the background poking through, a traveller
or two perhaps in a straw hat, neither
tea- nor wine-house close by, nor bordello,
or was I confusing cultures again,
and it seemed important that the mist was
not so pure as it had appeared at dawn,

that the autumn fires outside had been
giving up their smoke all day, offering
at the same time a simple solution
to the mystery of the missing leaves,
while the neighbours, in front of wood fires,
a little drunk on medicinal wine,
grappled with questions no less difficult
to answer, exhausted too from working
all day long to hold the apples steady
in the wisps of the trees, even as smoke
and mist worked to break our concentration
that kept the fruit solid, its colours true.

TANKA

Marianne Bluger

In the ruined orchard
among drenched leaves
I found you these
mist-silvered
fat blue plums

POOR MAN'S PINE

Julie Berry

grandma's rinsing warm blackberries
adding sugar
it's hotter'n the hubs of hell
something in grandpa's voice pounds the dark under the back
    porch
the beds upstairs are dreaming deserts
and the world raining and raining
when the needle sticks
hotter than   hotter than   hotter than

you can lead a woman to blackberries says grandpa
but you can't make her pick or blueberries neither
ugly enough to eat hay says grandpa
ugly enough
the kettle boils
grandma asks who
grandpa's on to aunt ellen's falsies
grandma's tight sweaters
slop bucket needs dumpin dad
grandpa hauls himself out of his chrome and plastic chair
six flies follow him out the door

land's so poor a rabbit'd hafta pack a lunch to cross it
paul who died so young would have loved that
as much as the oriole's nest by the railroad trestle over sunset
floating as he does between the line of norway spruce
and the falling down tobacco kiln
and me in the red corduroy dress that jim admired so
dancing backwards across fields
choked with poor man's pine

BLUEBERRIES, LUTICK'S FARM

Roger Bell

A gentle pressure of the thumb
tumble
into upturned palm
plump it
release your wrist so
they rumble
into the pail
at your waist
see it filling?
They have drunk the air
it's in their names
singing summer Canada
Patriot, the anthem
North Country
Northland
North Sky, blue
blue
gone deeper
St. Cloud, just that light
Blue jay, pinwheeling
calling through the pines
while dragonflies flit
and lean against the mesh
  Greg gives me to taste
  this, try this
  and this
  Friendship
  it is, too
  firm, round against my tongue
  the promise fulfilled
  the blue bond.

EDEN

Janice Kulyk Keefer

These blackberries you pour into my hands
know nothing of flaming swords
or cowed fig leaves. No word
for sin, salvation, in the language
milkweed speaks: whole clouds
of furred and dusky stars
nuzzle our feet—

The garden did no fall,
only grew wild again
so we might pick and eat
this fat-globed darkness, fire-sweet.

FROM WALTERS' VINEYARD

Slim Volumes

Aboard the back deck
we are Captains,
reckoning the hue of heaven
through raised glasses,
our noses windward
to the promise of
dung in melting soil.

Below, the eager earth
rolls and flows to slip
beneath flat Ontario's flood.

These waves of land
are parted
to counting-columns,

anticipating entries
of changing varieties,
of growth and decline,
of summer accumulations
to benchmarks worried
round Walters' winter table.

Into the legerdemain
is music writ,
(the measure borne
on timbre posts
—the bass construct of wine bars.)
Three blousey toilers
pitch upon a distant crest.
They string vines
on wire staffs,
to compose
where chords
of sweet round notes
will sail.

CHESTNUTS

Laurence Hutchman

We headed north in quest of chestnuts,
the last adventure of the summer before school began.
Up in the tree they appeared like sputniks.
With sticks we knocked them down,
split green leather rind to find grey-white nuts.
Later, we would harden them in the oven,
drill so as not to split the hole,
carefully thread with shoelaces
and take them into the schoolyard
for the conker battles,
to measure our victories in years.

Now, poring over these blank maps and concession lines,
the trees shine again on red brick houses in green fields.
At the end of our scavenger hunt
that encompassed the territory of dying farms,
we snuck up on the trees like cowboys in the grass.
I remember the tree on the Duncan farm,
the white curtains blowing into the form of a girl,
and the tree on Main Street where the Kilmers
played like gnomes among the ruined farm machinery.
I remember the tree by the Riley's white house
shimmering filaments in late August heat.

The most productive tree of all
stood between the Emery schoolhouse and the church
where sometimes we found chestnuts in the grass
and carried them to the stone war monument
where we broke the sharp shells open,
the spikes piercing the skin on our hands.
Afternoon's end and we headed home,
bulging chestnuts ripening in our pockets.

AT JIM McCONKEY'S FARM

Robert Sward

It's all quiet and we lie here numbered.
There is motion, rough-winged barn swallows
and clouds. Butterflies loop around one another
suggesting bows, configurations of a knot.
Both of us lose interest. The corrugated
galvanized roof of a 100-year-old barn
refuses light. The sun comes off it
in unexpected intensities. The fields and hills
form a backdrop to this. Cicadas and song sparrows.
The landscape rolls, my eyes roll with it.

Uneasily at first, unexpectedly it comes over me
that no one will ever not love here.
The new clothespins, the look of light on the line.
Old barns. Orchards. The John Deere harvester.
I am overwhelmed by the complexities
of skunk cabbage.

        It is warmish. The breeze pleases me.
Everything is dry. We stand and walk
around in the day. We walk out to the barn
with the corrugated top. Hours later we drink beer
and ponder the hollows under stars.
I have no thought whatsoever. I glance at her
and embrace her, but have nothing to say.
Implausible phrases, song titles, clichés—
        they come haltingly to mind.
Then the few convictions I have done well by.
We hold hands and walk around here.
No debts. No debts. Twelve years of manuscripts.
We can go in or out. At this moment,
for this day even, we have belonged here.
How did it happen? What have we affirmed?
We kiss the one star's lips. And always, married still
        we move on.

RED BARNS

John B. Lee

Last century
there was blood in the paint
on the boards of these barns.
Ontario, I have seen
the bleeding of a slaughtered sky
in the western hemorrhage
at the death of day
in the morbid menses
of a moon-timed afternoon
and thought of beauty dying
where it rubs the world away
in that the last of light
while somewhere else along the waking curve
young hours
warm the latches
on a dreaming door
and though a distant window sulks with rain
and pond mist
drifts like something burning slow
among the singing fogs
the blackbird's flashing wing
wags off the weed in flame
and dove flutes
mourn their flight
ah, moralizing angels, pass above these mortal barns
they bear the proof of lambs
gone silent on our knives
they have the memory of hog's lament
the sorrowing away
of market sows
the knackered beast
who proves his barrow's heart
is emptied as a well-squeezed rag
and all the sweeter crimson drums
have dripped dark zeroes full to the flux

that's quivered to final stillness in the ox
as thirsty cedar waits
to the very mow-boards
of these family farms
we've ghosts enough
to last us into unborn dust
make ashy berms from all romance
the fertile strangers yet to meet
and couple and decline
and this an awful art
behold the pigment of each generation's fate
red barns have much to expiate.

BARNSWALLOWS

David J. Paul

What I liked about
                     old man Bergman's barn
was not the chickenshit
                     the dust the chicken fluff
the sharpness of ammonia
                     the 40 kg bags of chicken feed
    lugged in my arms down
                     the steep and narrow wooden steps
  but the swallow nests
                     the muddy bowls
sticking to the rafters
                     littlebeaks of feathers
   poking curious air
                     the mother swallow
     treading water in
                     the square of Bateman light
wings slicing the sky
                     the definition of her name
    falling to the floor.

SURVIVAL

Grace Butcher

The brown chicken—fat old hen—
walks in the grass
sedately chicken-shaped,
surrounding young eggs of all sizes.

If she has thoughts,
they are bug-shaped, seed-shaped,
seen sideways through her round eyes.

Eggs slide out of her
when they are ready.

To go to bed, she flies
clumsily to a low branch
of the lilac bush,
not knowing why.

Darkness causes her eyes to close.

Beneath her in the same darkness
the fox jumps and jumps.

BARN'S DARK DOOR

Patrick Friesen

grain flies
in a perfect arc
from her hand
she is surrounded
by brown hens
and a red rooster

the sun is high
she wipes her brow
with the back
of one hand
wisps of white hair
at her temples

she looks at me
her eyes wrinkling
as she smiles
turning
and enters
the barn's dark door

OLD WHITE

Tony Cosier

As far removed as last New Year's
the old white looked as if
the knees would cave in under her.

Yet January first as younger horses
keep to the side of the barn
held by the sun's reflection off a wall,

she's out there in the open
compact in the wind
with a white mane angled to the blow

and the identical upright crumpled look
as she rolls a slow head back and forth
to tongue the snow from the hay.

PREMISES FOR A NEW ANIMAL HUSBANDRY

Jeff Seffinga

I   Destroy all rabbits first.

II   Any solid-coloured cow should be occasionally stroked to prevent anger and confusion. Stand back quickly if it seems you might violate her perception of her perfect frame.

III   To calm an overactive calf, take it by the ear and tail and hold it high in the air. When it no longer kicks or bawls, pull the tongue to hand from the left side of the mouth. Leave in a strawless black pen to meditate.

IV   Every piglet should be scrubbed and varnished with several coats so that its mother may not recognize it. Recitation of fairy tales before feeding will greatly increase its wisdom and moderate its temperament.

V   Sheep should be handled with the greatest care. Approach directly from the front, with hands outspread. It is advised to wear a simple cloak, woven of fine cotton and coloured with natural dyes. At the sound of a pure tone, it should stand still as if carved from living oak.

VI   Keep only black horses. Browns, dapples, and greys, may be fattened and delivered to be slaughtered. They are fit for consumption only if smoked or pickled. Beware the white horse; it harbors a historic curse.

VII   Dogs are seasoning, the secret ingredient in every recipe. Use sparingly to taste.

VIII   Cats are not animals.

HAIKU

Marianne Bluger

chores
in rose twilight—the quiet
jostle of sheep

A COW IN THE MUD LONG AGO

Derk Wynand

No one speaks or shouts. His voice does not suddenly crack. He does not raise his arm to call the attention of anyone else. No one shows much surprise at the time, which has nothing to do, he assumes, with the popular disregard for cows. The grass here along the dike grows too sparsely to tempt the domestic animals to graze. The tufts of camomile seem unpromising, the occasional patches of horsetail poisonous. Still, what does this bay of mud at low tide hold out to ruminants? Buried oysters, sharp and tough-shelled, hinged tightly shut? Every so often a starfish, cut or broken and, therefore, many-legged? Thin strands of an indefinable, surely inedible seaweed?

Far from shore, though not so far that its frightened bellowing cannot be heard, the cow has stumbled across a particularly treacherous spot of mud, where the consistency resembles that of quicksand. Where a child might safely walk, the heavier cow, on proportionately spindlier legs, sinks deeper. Now it rears up in the mud, shifting its centre of gravity toward its hindquarters, which settle in deeper. It shifts its weight forward and threatens to sink headfirst beneath the surface. It stops struggling, freezes, the panic only a dull glaze over its eyes, a resigned lowing that issues from its throat as though involuntarily. Now and again, it raises its head from the mud to bellow again, numbly, weak.

Soon the owner and his farmhands will arrive and assess the urgency of the predicament, and two of them will return to the barn to fetch the Clydesdales and the long rope and the boards for levering and prying. Even now, they manage partially to free the cow from the mud, enough to tie the rope around its neck. One of the farmhands begins to urge the Clydesdales forward, so that the rope loses its slack, and he shouts to keep the horses straining forward, and slaps their flanks with his hand, the rope always tighter. The cow, its forelegs sinking into the mud again, its head at an impossible angle and barely skidding along the mud's surface, utters no sound, the rope tight and tighter around its neck. If the animal struggles, the witness cannot distinguished its struggle from the jerking movements caused by the strain of the rope and the mud's resistance.

JOURNEY

Marilyn Gear Pilling

Down the path worn smooth by their feet
and the feet of the cattle
they come, every evening, these children
brother and sister, through the valley
across the log that spans
the creek, they walk the line between day
and night, the cattle dark
shapes against last light
scatter of grasshoppers, tremolo of
crickets, vibrato honk of a frog
just as they cross the log bridge,
jerk of water striders
on the surface below
flavour of creek, black muck
and wild mint, rail fence
slippery wet against bare legs.

Up the lane to the barn, they run
to meet buns of horse and pats of cow
straw, old stone and large warm beasts.
In the stable, corners and beams
hung with nests of swifts and spiders' silk
their Uncle's grip on the teat creates
a hard steady ping of milk on pail,
like a heartbeat or the hypnotic clop
of a horse's hooves.

Later on they emerge with the sealer
curved and warm, the milk washed blue
of the saltlick, these two,
down the lane, over the fence,
across the log, up the path
now dark, to home.

COWS

David J. Paul

Big-boned
and high-arsed
some always chewing,
the cows trundle
out of their mucky pasture
like old wooden carts.
Rich with milk
they do not trot,
their heavy udders
swaying almost painfully
between their hind legs.
The young woman
with the black wellingtons
and the obligatory stick
can not hurry them.
She smiles
at the stopped cars.
The cows' brown backs
rise and fall
like a dirty river
and they shit
when they feel like it,
cowplat, cowsplats
badging the road

as they amble on
instinctually, habitually
following their need,
sacred converters
of grass and givers
of milk.

TANKA

Marianne Bluger

Mad I stalk off
down the road in the teaming rain
& run out of steam
by a brook where plashing
cows seem quite content

COW FOR A DARK NIGHT

Cornelia Hoogland

In the Elora Gorge cows in waxy sunshine
stand in snow on the other side
of the wood-rail fence. We're skiing
the frozen river. Steam rises
from the flanks shiny as mink-oiled boots.
The cows, the boots. I think of you.

Your stained glass, rear-view
window in the library on Wortley. Cow flanks
in the stall at the Western Fair.
The cow's udder slopping between her legs.
Her milk's white echo in a galvanized pail.
Low thunder deep in her cow throat.

Here on the river heat rises
from the manure we smell
over the smell of new snow.

In your dark night, friend, this cow
for each of your five senses.
Stand in her warm accordion air.
Low to the earth she is deep
with meat. Your spiritual guide.

HAIKU

Marianne Bluger

my tire flat
the Holsteins calmly
turn to look

A COW ON THE BARDSTOWN ROAD

Marty Gervais

A man rides a truck
ahead of me from Bardstown
a cow in the back
shifting back and forth
with each new curve
of the road
its unsteady cow legs
doing a moon walk
on this clear afternoon

in March
I think of its sad cow eyes
drinking in the coming
of spring, of lush
pastures, of blue
skies, cumulus clouds
the warmth of earth
I think of its sad cow mind
speculating about change
and maybe about
the men and women
in the cars queuing up
behind this truck
and maybe about the
physics of speed
and sound and wind
along this road
I think of its sad cow eyes
dreaming of the earth
rushing by without her
A man rides a truck
ahead of me from Bardstown
adjusting the radio
heedless of the traffic
dreaming among the curves
of this road, eager to
bring home his new cow
eager to embrace
the promise of spring

WILL THE BULL

Marilyn Gear Pilling

On a short chain in the first stall
stood Will. We sidled past,
brushed against rough,
cool, cobwebbed stone
well away from his hooves.
His head turned sideways, one red eye
burned the cool gloom of the morning
stable, then a sudden sharp yank
on the chain by his urgent neck
sent us flying by. We knew Will was
father to every calf, husband
to every cow, this the cause of his
blue-murder intentions.

When Will was out, we crossed fields
the long way, never far
from the fence, not fooled
by the droning afternoon, the harmless
sun, the dawdle of small, white, butter —
flies. Within leap of the fence
we crossed fields hoping
for the glitter of Will's magic stick,
to dash straight across risked
ram trample gore.
                 Beneath us
ran faultlines; a heave or a throw,
and the earth could split open
                       in those fields
the common sowthistle, the most homely ragwort
trembled in the anticipation of a god.

BILLY AND THE RAT

Hugh MacDonald

I don't know who set that trap
(One of those steel-jawed things
that could bite
off a small boy's hand
like a buzz saw).
Billy and I found it
upstairs in the granary
in a trough
in a sea of oats,
when it jumped in the air,
as we passed it by
kicking a scatter of grain
across our startled backs.
The rat clamped
in its rusted maw
was young and scared.
Be careful, it could bite,
I said as Billy picked it up
and set it on the bench
along the wall.
"He's too hurt," he said
and opened up the trap.
Are you gonna kill it?
"No," he said, "His leg is broken.
He'll likely die
without my help.
You stay here
and watch him."
The rat lay
on the bench,
and watched me,
with squirrel eyes;
his round tummy
rose and fell.
Billy brought sticks

and baler twine.
I watched him splint
the rat's leg
and hide him
where Grampy wouldn't look.
Every day we fed him
milk from a dropper
and bits of bread
talked to him
and touched him
like a pet.

The day the splint came off
Ratty was growing strong.
And maybe it hurt him
when we untied the string,
made him lose his temper
and bite Billy
inside the thumb
where the skin is webbed
like a bat's wing.
Before Billy could think
his big hands moved fast,
fingers strong
from milking cows
snapped that young rat's neck.
and dropped him to the floor.
"Damn stupid rat," he said,
and ran crying
out the door.

LONG TIME GONE

Eugene McNamara

The last light falls on mossy
gravestones the names already
blurred with snow —

I've been a long time gone —

I'm back here now and snow
falls on a horse's back he
moves away from the fence
between breaths and still
snow moves with him across
the field —

Everything has come back here
among the stones where things
end and begin to hurt —

It was a day of long shadows
and a long drive past fields
full of frost on the corn
shocks — a long time —

No use to call the horse
I don't know his name or
remember the names of those
already gone —

I stand still in the silence
thinking:

I would not have missed it
for the world but who will
see it after me?

I've been a long time gone —

DEAD HORSE WINTER

Jim Green

He made it back to the ranch
in two long days, snow piled
three feet when he left town,
covered the top wires
by dawn next morning
as he leap-frogged along
with two worn out horses
lunging chest deep in drifts.

The cattle were bawling
bunched up in the creek bed,
sucked them out with the smell
of loose hay and a trail
punched through by the Clydesdales
dragging the sled. He set out
next day for the horses
but his mounts bogged down
just short of the ridge.
He stuck his saddle in a tree
sent the horses on the backtrail
and floundered on alone
with snowshoes made of aspen,
strips from a grey blanket
and strings from the saddle.

The last days were the worst,
searching the still canyons
for stranded wasted bands,
the killing   blood
splattered on crystal white,
the numbing slam of the rifle
and the screams.

The lucky ones were dead
already, the rest almost gone,
slumped walleyed in soft snow
just slack hide and hard bones.
They had no tails left and
even manes were missing where
they'd chewed on each other.
Sticks poked through
slashed cheeks, gums raw
bloodied from crushing branches,
the last of the feed.
He shot and kept shooting,
killed a hundred and more
first with the long gun
till he ran out of shells,
finished the last of them off
with an old Savage shotgun.

In the spring a gelding
with eight gaunt mares in tow
came down from the valley,
survived the snow.

THE BEAUTY OF PIGS

Jeff Seffinga

Strong and eager, filled
with a sap that was part hope
but more determination, he came
a young man to this young land
bringing wife and babies.
With only a peasant's education
he sought out labour, let slide
what others considered opportunity:
the fancy car, his own home,
the lure of business partnerships.
He let those chances pass him by,
foolishly (people thought) devoted
his efforts to the well-being of family
and the raising of pigs. His father had
always claimed a man's honour
lay in the beauty of animals.

He began with a rented decrepit barn
and four piglets bought at auction,
fattened them inexpensively
on table scraps and the collected
vegetable waste from supermarkets
and restaurants, brought home
on a hand-made cart and boiled up
in five-gallon pails on the kitchen stove.
Without question his wife and children
helped with the work even at times
when they suffered the sneers,
derisive words about pig farmers
aimed and flung to hurt like arrows.
Tolerated only a little bit more
than beggars and tramps, the family
lived for each other, almost outcast.

His elegant neighbours, in their scorn
were unaware how his dedication
and the family's hard work
turned a spurned activity into
the fulfillment of a dream that they
could not imagine, until he had gathered
money for his own farm, until the pigs
won ribbons and awards nationally.
For when his name was known
in all the important places of power
they clapped his back, offered advice
and invitations into their circles.
He'd listen and smile, but placed his faith
in the true source of his power:
his wife and children, the shared belief
in the proud beauty of pigs.

THE CLIFFS BANK SHARPLY HERE

Cornelia Hoogland

I have a question for the goat spine
chucked carelessly on the rubbish heap
I stumble across after the Quaker meeting in Sparta
while looking for Hawk Cliff but finding
on the far point of land
in a farmer's stubble field at the edge of Lake Erie
this dump.

The path of loving the earth I like to think
I'm on is through junked
canvas, garbaged life
(this jacket might have saved a life
on Erie), rubber tires, hooped
bedsprings, and the goat

skull peppered black
with flies on the still-fleshy bones.
Will an apology suffice? Dear Goat
let me explain about human beings...

Around the garbage stand simple trees.
Burnished leaves toss their gold
and die with a faithfulness
this morning's Christian hymns
didn't come close to understanding.
Bad death/good death,
like trying to put this and that together,
is all the same vanity.
Even earth's ruly spine banks sharply here
where the cliff tears clay hunks of flesh,
like a woman eating herself,
into the dark hall of the lake.

THE SOUTHWEST SASKATCHEWAN BADGER
William Robertson

What it comes down to for the old badger
is pushing his oxygen tank through the Swift Current mall
and giving shit to a sixty-five year old
who's quit farming:
what the hell, says the retiree
I've got enough to live on and you can't
take it with you
which is exactly what the old badger
had planned, the legendary tightwad
who scrounged worn tires from us at the shop
to outfit his augers and balers
who wore rubber boots and rope belts
who saved his wife and kids
from spending a cent and saved it all

to walk the mall, sucking Medicare oxygen
and swearing at senior citizens
who take three-day trips to North Dakota
to lose a hundred dollars on the roulette wheels
while their wives buy the grandchildren t-shirts,
extravagant bastards who've betrayed
the sheer pleasure of saving money
and screaming at some young teller
for tacking on a 50-cent service charge

he shakes his head at his profligate friend
and carries on up the walkway
window-shopping and barely able
to draw his next breath, fists clamped tight
now he's cornered by his health
and these crazy ways of doing things
moving on the memory of every dollar
he's ever made, where he keeps it,
knowing it will save him
from the bad times to come
he's been waiting for
all his gleefully miserable life.

MOMENTS THAT STOP THE NIGHT

Brother Paul Quenon

Coyote wail
through the cold darkness
and silence the thoughts
of the hermit.

* * *

"Strangeness! Strangeness!"
the owl cries to
the frosted world

lit by the moon.
"Strangeness! Strangeness!"
The awaking monk says:
"That's a dog howling."
and goes back to sleep.

        * * *

The muffled low of a cow
sends mother-comfort
to the hermit asleep
under the full moon.

      * * *

How is it the owl,
in the frozen depth of night,
sounds so soft and warm?

IOWA CITY, IOWA
"Some years the ground pulls harder – "

Robert Sward

He mounts his tractor.
There are creatures in trees
whose names I do not know.
There are others in procession before us.
Pigs the size of buffalo. Cattle
the tails and markings of horses.
Iowa. What am I doing in Iowa?
Ann lies in the sun. Dozing. Depressed.
Stripping, rising on my hind legs,
hairy, cloven-footed,
Centaur, I declare myself: Centaur.
Then chicken. Then horse. Bull. Then pig.
Let us plant our dreams.
Write them down and plant them.

Plant sugar cubes.
Make love.
Then dig it up, turn it over
and plant the ground,
that ground we made love on.
What will grow there?
Rhubarb.
A peach tree.
The ground holds me as I make love to it.
How is it birds no longer fly?
Horses only. The entire state of Iowa.
What about deities,
these deities that eat your brains?
And why anyway should I mind that?
I am busy planting my brains.
I will harvest them remind me please before leaving.
The time has come.
O look Centaur   Snowing   Your eyes
your eyes
they touch me.
I have been asleep.
Does it hurt?

BECAUSE HE FACES LEVIATHAN

Betsy Struthers

Struggling to shift the plow through caked red dirt, ox
straining at the lead. Clatter of hooves sounds the alert:
pilot whale stranded in the river. But the name he hears
is *Pilate*, washing his hands with dust. Oh, *the vanity
of all things here below which gave me such a longing
to go forth*...and with such fear.

   He simply leaves the poor beast hobbled there,
head bent to the dry ground, and runs barefoot over fields

and dykes. Crowd gathered on the shore, stalled by that
black bulk. Some of the men hold hooks. Scythes, saws.
Women with knives and pans. Even the children lower
their loads of wood, frozen in their place. *Shall one
not be overwhelmed at the sight of him?**
      Leviathan weeps once more, an eerie whistle
echoes between hills, rises rises falls. The mouth
that would swallow Jonah closed to him. The eye.
Window of the soul. His own soul *raised...*
with groans and earnest cries. Still he stands
on the brink. Apart from his neighbors. As if
in the belly of the fish. In such darkness. His lungs
burn, his throat, his fluid breath, drained by tide's retreat.

*Job 41:9

FARM POEMS

James Reaney

Boreen

Lane
farm
born.
Biked, walked
to being taught
in town.
In winter
deep, deep snow
because
Our neighbour, Halpin,
when my grandfather
went to Ulster
in 1912,
Moved his line fence close over.
So
often impassable
1/2 mile to house
isolated, lonely,
but a big part of my education!
The lane moved beside me
As my thoughts moved inside me—
Ruts, brickbats, chokecherry,
Puddles, wild apple tree
bend
3 old maples
poplar
gateway
The Gravel Road
On the way to school
That taught me Latin
But
Never anything so dear
As Lane

Lahey

The Irishmen whose five farms
Were all connected to the Huron Road
By this long, long lane,
They called the boreen.
Started by Michael Lahey in 1842
Over Daly's 25 acres — back, back south
Unto a hillock overlooking a cedar swamp
Where he cleared room for a log house,
Its hollow still to be seen and
Fragments of its dishes
Picked up from ploughing.
Also, a wife, Catherine, six kids,
Two oxen, 20 acres of wheat
40 bushels of potatoes and three pigs.

Two farms east, Catherine scrubbed floors
For Wilfrid Thompson past whose house
Daily a stage struggled
To the village of Stratford.
On one St. Patrick's Day, Michael,
Who worked for Thomas was fired
— Riotous behaviour — drunk.
In 1865, Michael divided the farm,
His hundred acres, into 50 acres west
For his son Michael; 20 acres southeast
For James, 20 acres east for Thomas, and
Ten acres left for himself and wife:
All this connected by twisting through
Swamp and swale and hollow and boreen
Which also served neighbour Halpin —
To church, to market, to mill, to court!

Reaney

When my grandfather started thinking of this farm
It was divided in two between an Irishman named Quirk,
Brother-in-law to Marty Halpin, the line fence mover,
And a brick maker, Roberts: Quirk's orchard stuck out
Into Roberts's brickyard 1/2. Roberts drank,
Beat his wife, was mayor of Stratford, wore
Copper bracelets on his arms, copper earrings,
All to keep off the rheumatism.
Right on top of Lahey's original clearing,
Roberts dug a clay pit called the "clay hole"
This resulted in a brickyard whose workers
Came in the long lane by the fence,
Brickbats, white clay pipes, broken too,
Smoking kilns.
Slowly the clay pit filled with water,
Bankruptcy, but still the colossal stumps
Of the cedar trees Lahey had sawed sit upside down
Thinking to themselves in the water of the Clay Hole.

Farmwork

I remember picking mustard in James Lahey's field.
I, in early poem, called it "heretic lollard weed."
When plowing, a riding plow, I also carried
In my pocket, a copy of Paradise Lost where
All the f's were s's unless they came at the end
of a word. My stepfather picked it up where it had
Fallen into a furrow! Plowing went like this:

Harrowing went like this:

======================================

======================================

======================================

======================================

On Michael Lahey Jr's East Fifty.
On his parents' 10 acres, I hoed 85 rows of turnips.
On Quirk's front field of 25 acres which he bought
From Daly, I built, with a fork, 200 stooks of wheat,
And read Thomas Hardy's Jude the Obscure.
Every morning at 6 a.m. I rose up to call in the cows:
Named Josephine, Blossom, and Cherry &c. Cowpaths
these dear beasts had made with their feet
Were as incredible as the long lane made by Lahey.
They took account of the lay of the land.
On Saturday, I chased after horses
For the riding academy we had for a while.
Roy was our cleverest—would open granary door
With his teeth and jump fences. Favourite memory
Is watching a caterpillar tractor,
Completely out of control, lumbering
Across a field, through Cardwell's line fence.
If I can do it for someone else I like,
I don't mind farming.

The Lane Again

In three quarters of an hour I am to play
A Beethoven Sonata at the Music Festival
Up town in the City Hall. At the very end
of the lane my bicycle tumbles into a puddle
As do I and I have to race back to the house
For my second best suit; arrive with five minutes
To go. I wouldn't have any of this any other way!

GREAT GRANDMOTHER'S WELL

David J. Paul

The well is a hole
in the earth down
which I could fall
shocked and screaming
into my own small
and shrinking death
a splashing in a drowning
claustrophobia.
My approach over the
jigsawed quarry stones
is slow, circuitous,
careful. I never draw
water. I only watch
the silver bucket drop
like a hanged man
and then I peer down
clutching to the small
walled edged and hear
its dangling creaking
fading and see my
self in the wrong
end of a telescope
playing in the sky
like child and god.
The pail rises heavy
as a stone heavy as
the reluctance of earth
to give up its own
the water slopping
the rope coiling like
a snake around a
drum and the gift
of water wrinkling there
silver and laughing
except for the horrible

reach across the wellmouth
to grab the bucket
and pour its life
into a pitcher.

HORIZON RESEEDS WHILE A COMBINE CRYSTALLIZES AND THE WHEAT WALKS UP AND BANGS ON THE STOCKADE GATE

Charles Noble

In mid-August the ship-like John Deere
pull-type combines used to be hauled out,
carefully spaced in the yard,
a road scribbled into a sizeable courtyard
surrounded by Quonset, garage, shop,
barn, elevator, bunkhouse, house.

Chains were checked, bearings looked at,
concaves and cylinder teeth maintained,
pick-up tines replaced, canvases unravelled,
new slats riveted.

Wrenches lay in the powdered dirt
like squawking bird beaks,
legs wrestled out of life into death snapshots
stuck out from around five-foot wheels.

Weed and wheat blood stained
the canvas. Above the hedges
a tapestry appeared just before noon,
yellow orange brown and black harvest
in the washed-out sky
behind which were miles of eye-gnawing chaff.
At dinner the sky turned bluer
over the burnished stubble and gone stalks

barnacling the dinner-to-dinner combines.

In the field, wrinkled and dusty,
the number two combine stopped,
bearing gone and fan hitting its housing
into hole. Horizon flared up, then whipped away.
Blood into the eyes to the hands
swallowed back separated hunger.
The foreman came out with the half-ton
and they set up tapestry screens,
went to work welding with afternoon starlight.

IN THE FALL I REMEMBER

Anne Compton

In the fall I remember
an abundant life in a large house:
we were a crowd, a country, a state.
Done, doing and yet to do — work without end,
work named by the hour, the day and the season —
a marshalled life.

My father did everything, was everything-
lord of our lives — a cursing, gentle man.
He could parse and he could scan,
line a psalm, recite a poem, build a barn.
For him we took each meal in silence —
eleven children, and always the visitors:
his rule.

Every room full and attics stowed,
halls without heat and winter stoves;
and below
in the cool dark cellar
jars of jam, red as cardinals and gold-capped.

In the well-house, pickled hams and dried fish,
and twice a week, the baking.

A life banked against winter.

THE DIGGING OF DEEP WELLS

Hugh MacDonald

involves
the breaking of solid ground,
stacking a circle's worth of sod
between tree stumps,
shovelling layers
of damp and musty clay,
into wooden pails,
and soon requires
a ladder, and a tripod
of white-barked birch,
and where it's joined
a wooden block
through which passes
a hundred feet
of sturdy rope.
Then begins
the lining of walls
—fresh cut sandstone
starts ten feet down,
builds up layer by layer
tight to the top.
Since there's no sign yet
of gurgling water,
the digger digs anew
goes down inside
the present ring of rock
with short armed spade,

sharp and heavy crow,
hammers stubborn aggregate
smashes layered shale,
load after deadly load
sways up behind the rope.
The lower he goes,
the harder falling pebbles hit,
the deeper the darkness.
At ladder's length
more layered circles of stone,
hole gradually widening
until this present wall
provides foundation
for the wall above
and by lantern light
the digger stands
on broken rock,
watches the ladder rise
and disappear above the rim.
The air is chill:
each clatter of crow
each scrape of shovel
each claustrophobic breath
echoes up the hole
toward the light
past the rain of dust
that coats the chilling sweat
of neck and brow.
And now at end of work
the bucket ends its day,
is swift unbound,
replaced by bosun's chair,
twirling he rises, to sleep
and then descend again
and again
until one afternoon
he stands in icy damp
hears the gush of stream

and fresh cold water rise up,
shock his weary groin.
Filled up with sudden joy
he risks to look
at what's above
and finds as his reward
a perfect circus of stars

LAUNDRY, NEAR PHELPSTON

Roger Bell

From the sky have fallen blue
and white clouds whip
flap on the long line
the west wind tugs a hem
urges
Come back
to the day
before the sun
empties you
 but the farmer's wife
has pegged them tight
and cut off their wings
with a caning knife
and now along the thinness taut
they can only lean
and yearn

NO MORE BABUSHKA PLOWING DEMONSTRATIONS

Steven Michael Berzensky

in this invasion of grandmothers
how many of you resembled mine

same solemn Slavic features
(those familiar orthodox Jewish faces)
same strong Ukrainian hands
(that weathered skin those stout bodies)

and yet I had never seen
a holy army of babas before

you the old women
were wearing your heavy black workshoes long plain dresses
and babushka scarves
wrapped like crescent moons
around your chins and ears

you were pulling together an old wooden plow
gripped by a man
over soil and weeds and stones
digging hard furrows in the field

but especially you
the woman in the lead
straining in your harness diminutive as an angel
your delicate bones
not yet broken

we were told this is how it was
in Old Mother Russia
in the pioneering days
on the Canadian prairies

yes it was only a demonstration

but I witnessed it yesterday
in Yorkton Saskatchewan
and I saw you
the eighty-year-old leader
your white socks falling to your ankles
as you stamped your shoes upon the earth
the globes of salty sweat
pouring down your reddened face
and I thought
she's going to have a heart attack
and I wanted to shout
Stop

but no one would hear me
in the cheering neck-craning awe-struck crowd

maybe I was mistaken

maybe this plowing demonstration
is a neglected form of exercise
to be recommended
for all octogenarians
    (of both sexes)

or maybe it's a necessary ritual
of suffering and endurance
preparing us each
for the blessings of heaven

or maybe it's merely
another chunk of evidence
this crazy world
is crazy for eternity

O babushkas
O grandmothers
O workhorse angels

O serene old women
serving as substitutes for oxen

tell us the truth

if we never see you again
on earth will this also mark the end
of all babushka plowing demonstrations
in the fields of heaven

FREE ASSOCIATIONS ON FAIRY TALES
Jack and the Beanstalk, Part II

Ronnie R. Brown

She is tearing up
an old bed sheet. Ripping
strips that will soon
tie tomato plants, heavy
with bounty, to the stakes
she's fashioned out of branches,
victims of last season's ice storm.
Her daughter, ancient
at twenty three, can not understand
why she wastes her time this way.
Why all this ripping and whittling
when garden stores sell
everything—all sorts of plastic
this and that—which her daughter *knows*,
will work better, look nicer.

One day, years from now
when her daughter has grown younger
she will tell her about the hours
she spent as a child helping
her mother and grandmother, of the countless

generations of women; the untold
hours of tearing, whittling, staking, weeding
picking, cooking, canning, serving.
Explain how every time
she drives a stake, ties
a beanstalk she
can almost see the family
farm her grandmother used to describe, hear
the voices of all the women
who came before
urging her
on.

THE OLD FARM WOMAN EXAMINES HER THOUGHTS

Grace Butcher

What comes through now
is the quarrel and twitter of guinea hens,
the sudden noise and muttering of the white ducks,
the sawing apart of the air by the roosters.

From the warm dark of the barn
comes the velvety nicker of the old horse;
the cats tease and twist around my legs.

I have become a good herder of chickens.
If they do not head for the coop by dusk,
I walk behind them quietly and skillfully
and move them towards sleep.

Powerfully I climb the vertical ladder
to the hayloft, toss the sweet hay
easily through the small opening.

The cats dash between my footsteps,
but my feet go always to the right spot.

Now what am I to do with all these skills?
My choice was to be here alone,
to move through time of my own choosing,
to weave this place around me so tightly
no one could get in.

But the fence posts rot;
the horse breaks out whenever he wants;
the chickens are in the neighbour's field;
the cats go down the road;
the ducks make their own lakes
every time the rain falls;
the guinea hens fly clear to the rooftops.

I might as well let some people in.
I don't really have to do chores
as often as I say I do.
And I must remember to listen.
Not everyone cares to know
how many eggs were laid today,
or that there's this duck
who's in love with me.

Oh, what *does* one talk about, anyhow?
Already I hear the sound of voices
coming up the lane.

LOOKING FOR HOME

Robert Currie

With Grandma in the passenger seat
and between us the worn photocopy
of a Cummins rural directory map,
we head for the northwest quarter
of section 6, township 14, range 28,
west of the 2nd meridian, the home place.
Driving west from Moose Jaw, we pass a blaze
of ripe canola, a brief blue haze of flax,
then, leaning with the wind, miles of wheat,
dry as sunlight, smooth fields running together,
section after section flowing from the horizon.
"Look at it now," she says. "You'd never guess
the fight we had, just to break this land."
She directs me higher, into the Coteau hills.
"Good plan," I say. "We can get our bearings
when we spot Johnstone Lake."
"Johnstone," she says, "he was just a flabby English lord,
on holidays, played at being a buffalo hunter."
She turns and glares at me. "The name, the only name,
is Old Wives' Lake."

She tells the story she heard as a child.
Cree people, after food and far from home,
attacked by Blackfoot warriors, fought them off
till sundown. Knew more would come at dawn.
"The old women weren't good for much,
scraping hides, cutting and drying meat."
Grandma's voice firm, her hands shaking with palsy.
"But they could make a difference. It was their plan
to circle the carts and camp the night.
At daybreak, when the Blackfoot struck,
all the young had slipped away,
creeping by dark through the coulees,
heading home toward Qu'Appelle.
The braves found only women to kill, old wives,

74

grandmothers, they killed them all."
She pauses, her eyes alight with other lives.
"When the wind blows on the lake,
you can hear them wailing in the night.
Sometimes you can see their shawls,
caught in the briars, like great white birds
resting in the brush of the island."
We see the lake below us then,
a bright splash in August sunshine.
"It's alkalai," she says, "bitter as tears."

She points. "That's where your people lived."
I turn the car onto a dirt trail,
bouncing in old ruts, till she signals.
"Here. This is it." She swings wide the door,
stands, turning slowly to stare,
wheat swaying at her waist.
At last she speaks. "I was born right here."

There is no house, no barn, no sign
of shed nor shack, not a scrap of wood.
In the surge and billow of bending grain
a dip where once the cellar was.
She shakes her head. "All the work, "she says,
"and now, who would know or care?"

Her gaze swims through the waves.
"Shut your eyes," she says, "and listen.
It's as if we'd never been. None of us.
The same as always, nothing but wind."

Eyes closed, a breath of wind on my face,
I feel the past stir around us, hear
the weary murmur of farm women
resting at last in the dark,
the sigh of a mother whose children
are safe at home for the night.

STONEY LAND

Patrick Friesen

lean and stark apart,
striding across the stubbled earth,
the old man knew the hairs of sorrow.
each knuckle of his hands a fist,
each finger a bent direction.

(he knew the plod of a slow horse
with dust like chaff at its feet,
the Sunday chat of hens
making a stillness in the barn.)

and he knew the clatter of clay
on a box, where his woman lay.

his mouth a wound,
his voice harsh
and his words graceless,
he sat gaunt in his straight chair,
unlamenting.

ETYMOLOGY OF PROGRESS
Penn Kemp

Nobody told my grandmother
who prepared for the event
as the year's swell festival.

She drove the buggy to town
for music and edification away
from the champion cattle, out of
the rolling fields she was born to.

Ontario, the Iroquois word for
Beautiful. From forest to farm,
the rich black loam now
asphalt sparkling on the road.

She warned me against gypsies
and Indians camping down creek
who would steal me for a changeling.
If I didn't watch out.
I watched out, wanting.

Nobody told her Chautauqua meant
the place where one was lost.

FATHER

Marilyn Gear Pilling

On this path familiar
as the curves and mounds
of my body, this path that bends
past plump hills secret with tunnels,
among trees of thorn whose limbs are webbed,
where cornflowers tap my ankles and
blue shells of robin eggs scatter,
always I am looking for you.

> this is the farm you called
> The Other Place, here was neither
> house nor barn, we were forbidden
> to speak of this farm. Here
> was your war. You hacked thorn trees
> burned tent caterpillars, drove your car
> to gopher holes, poured exhaust
> down tunnels. You strung
> a fence along the high banks

of the river, on my thigh is a
scar from the barbed wire.

This day, I leave the path
follow a side trail through
long grass to a pond that will be gone
by summer, in the sponge of mud at its border
hundreds of frogs the size of thimbles,
lucent golden frogs with sticky,
delicate feel.

Are these the froggies that
never knew a story or a rhyme at all?
Will I free you if I catch them,
if I kiss them as they fly one
by one through my fingers?

BECAUSE HE DANCES ON
THE EDGE OF THE ABYSS

Betsy Struthers

Arms crossed over his chest, bare
feet stamping the earth in a
rhythm wild as the French fiddler's
jig can take him. His companions
match his steps, pour him another
glass of dandelion wine, mug of
spruce beer. *Carnal pleasure:* heart
beating so fast the room pulses
with heat, bodies weaving together
in reels they urge him to lead as he
loves to lead, commands the
shivaree on his sister's wedding
night, drum of sticks, panting

flutes (John in his shirt at the
opened window and Mary behind
him, hair loose, lips swollen). He
flees the *frolick*, afflicted by these
*dreadful views, the gulph of
perdition beneath my feet;* runs
frantic into the night fields, to
weep, to pray away the sin he
yearns for, fist in his teeth.
Cinnamon fronds of barley
bend over him where he lies,
face down, hugging the
dirt that claims him *for
dust you are, and to dust
shall you return.**

* *Genesis 3:19*

HIATUS

Dorothy Sjoholm

the evening light is tender
the snow deep and soft
only the hard-packed track of the toboggan
reveals our presence

her voice calling us home for supper
too soon
eclipses this hiatus

too soon
this light will be replaced
by blazing summer days
with scorched brown soil
and stubble-scratched shins

smeared with dirt and blood
eyes and nose will burn
in air fouled
by the chaff and dust of the threshing machine
in endless heat the summer kitchen
will struggle
to feed
men in from the fields
and in the afternoon
our hoes will chop through rows
of eternal weeds   and turnips
sweat stinging our heat-glazed eyes

but now
appalled by my own bravado
I lurch forward
down the steep bank
hurtle along the track
that bridges the ditch and crosses the road beyond
the sentry
now off duty
pulls her sleigh through rose-coloured snow
up the long laneway
toward the lighted house
while I
still thrilled with the terror of the flight
drift to a stop
in the middle of Concession # 8

THE CHILDREN ON THE ROAD

Robyn Sarah

The children on the road, looking for fool's gold
among the scattered gravel, soon leave behind
the farmhouse with its west-facing porch blind
drawn against the late sun. Evening cold
breathes from the dense bush. They're gripped by an old
passion—each bent head fervent to find
the perfect crystal kindled in the mind.
Long into dusk, the search exerts its hold.

Long into dusk (unmindful of our calling)
they run, they stoop, sift gravel through their fingers,
cry out to one another—their urgent voices
drifting to where we dream. (Slow shadows falling
aslant the porch quench the last gold that lingers.)
Long into dusk we sit, plumbing our choices.

NOVA SCOTIA VACATION

William Robertson

The village lunatic screams obscenities
back into the store's quiet darkness
as we walk up. He holds the screen door
carefully for "Ma'am" then "Sir."
On the step a kid going into
grade six, with nothing to do but
wait for it, watches the water run
from our car's air conditioner
onto the empty street. Inside
a sad man whose family has
owned this store for over fifty years,
selling the place by bits, waits

for the service station down the road
to close, for his neighbour's kid out front
to grow up and go, for us
to quit asking questions
and leave.

SCATTERBRAIN GATHERS

Charles Noble

I sit in the kitchen as my brother asked
and it is cool
the fields on the table
are next to my heart
and the list of machinery
is growing into the world
where the gentle lawyer, a minister's son
my mother remembers from high school,
is unfolding the law
into our hands.

My brother has carefully listed
all the machinery and their present values
which I will read over the phone
to the lawyer who gives us the picture,
the sister's liquid settlement
and tax implications for my mother.

On the same table is a beautiful field
plan drawn up by my brother
just like my father used to do,
his field plans for years past underneath,
together on a clipboard.

The old machinery parked in the alternate
garden plot behind the hedge
but then hedged again
has weeds and trees growing into it.
We buried my grandfather between
two old combines.

In the house practically empty of furniture
I wait for the lawyer to call back.
I read over the list: trucks, tractors,
loaders, to odds and ends
still valuable but unrealized a loss
among the rusted junk like jewelry
on the suckers of the photosynthetic kingdom
rooted, and burning at both ends.

I think of my father whose brain
will allow only swear words
from the right hemisphere.
His brother rents out the south side
of the farm to a neighbour.

These tractors were pulling for us,
a drawbar seance.
Now the restless, irregular calling
is distilled
and the table moving.

SNOW DOWN HOME

Eugene McNamara

They tell strangers not to
try to get to the mailbox
in a storm many have tried
gone and died on the way—

That snow is confusing
like God gone nuts—

Come summer and corn
tassels hang in sunshock
you remember the snow
and almost miss it—

Take the hired man who
showed up at harvest
time worked my uncles
field ate dinner with
the family didn't say where
he had been nobody asked—

After the harvest he up
and left next fall he
didn't come back nobody
asked where he was where
he had gone—

Like someone who went out
in the blizzard trying
to find the barn or go
back home just went out—

WALKING BETWEEN FIELDS

Hugh MacDonald

edging evergreen woods
my Grampy
picks and points
and I listen
more to the murmur
of his voice

than the import
of his words.
He names everything
plants, trees, animals,
insects, birds, fungi,
footprint, feather, rock,
talks of characteristics,
usefulness, dangers,
season, beauty,
nuisance and charm.
The sun shines warm
across our shoulders
birds serenade
and insects hum.
He tells me to remember
all he names
and I say I will...
I remember still
his softness of voice
the smell of his pipe
the shapes and colours
where we walked,
his guiding hand
and pointing finger,
but not a single word,
a solitary name.
I wish I did
and yet I know
now who I am,
and that
if I walked
with him again
I'd do the same.

THORLEY

Glynn A. Leyshon

Grizzled, stoic and taciturn,
Face like an axe blade;
lean as a hoe handle
And just as tough
Old Man Thorley always hid his eyes
With a straw hat
In the fields with his pickers
Always doffed it at the house
For grace and eating
Showing an upper brow of
Baby white, yielding and soft.
Sharp as a sliced melon against
The brown of his face.
Steeled to fatigue and discomfort,
Thorley worked harder than all of us
Pickers combined even with
His elbow cocked at right angles
Like a dog's hind leg—
Result of a fall as a kid.
The elbow, though, made him a magician
With the signal flags in the "other war."
Too old for this one, he joined
the RHLI reserve—the RILEYS
and when they hit the beach at Dieppe
He was in the tomato field.
A neighbour passed the news
Of dead and wounded in their hundreds.
Thorley stood rigid with pride and wonder
Then tears fought out
from under his hat
"Isn't it grand," he whispered.

URGENT THINGS
FOR C.H.

John B. Lee

How we learn
if we live long lives
about the rhythms of a lifetime —
and I add to urgent
and important things, *necessity*
and make of this
a wise enough completion
to satisfy, at least for now

and just a while ago
I sat on the cement verandah
near the gone
redolence of wild current
stolen from June
by the men on the farm
who rip things out
and my mother said
aren't we three old fools
of herself and my father and uncle
we'll work til we drop
and I see
by the stagger of shadows
in a balance of pails
how half-oat heavy they are
how the peach crop comes and goes
unattended.
I remember the greenings
fallen to a brown bruise
on a cider-scented wind
touching the world by dozens
as they disappear
as then I know
my father must sell the sheep

a hundred years
since they came here first
and *all things come to an end* he says
and I feel
his sadness as you would
a coolness on a sunlit stone
under the slow drag
of shade
and of this *necessity*
of the fecklessness of true seeing
when things begin to blur
as it is with the memory of dreamers
fading into wakefulness

and as a boy
impatient over everything
not centred on myself
I was so wonderfilled
the light came off me
in a wash
where now it settles in
on my father's hearing
a dark absorbing sorrow silenced
by the bleating hills.

FAMILY GATHERINGS

Wayne Lanter

The stories were always steeped in runic tones,
not quite myth,
the plodding truths of yeomen's dialogue,
but no more probable than Lazarus,
of cows plucked from rumination
and lifted over telephone wires,
the walking on water wonder
of a tractor trailer truck transported
to the other side of a lake,
its wheels creating a transcendental wake
of water and wind, to be set down
in the middle of a plowed field,
the driver in the cab, miraculously, unharmed.
Or, a giant stone from the south pasture
uprooted and rolled into the road
as if by plan, and left there
almost as a challenge to good sense,
that took twelve men
three days to break up and clear away.

Uncles, fathers, sons, small, lean
and hungry looking men, cousins,
husbands and husbands-to-be,
an occasional bachelor nephew,
an alien brother-in-law,

on some not too well understood holiday
like the Fourth, or Good Friday,
or the Sunday before a Monday Memorial Day
that wasn't Memorial Day at all,
would sit at the open end of the garage,
cradling cans of beer,
smoking cigarettes and pipes.

It was a listing of connections.

but without a core, a vacuum in a funnel,
a family gathering laced up tightly
and held in place as if each had ordained
the genetic order from which it came.
It was a council for the impossible,
as if each had chosen existence
over all the other possibilities,
all agreeing, shaking their heads,
not in opposition to the verities
but simply at the wonder of it.

And because all things are possible
in a vacuum of belief or disbelief,
there was a story about three pieces of straw
hammered into a Cottonwood tree,
hammered in like railroad spikes
upon which to hang any number
of theories about how things happen.

At the other end inside the house,
tilted away from the men only slightly,
chairs backed to the living room walls
to reinforce the keep, aunts, in their girth
and weight small Conestoga wagons,
set up for the night, red with the blood
that nourished the moons of their faces,
the pennants of their lace handkerchiefs
waving now and then in the oppressive air,
infants on the floor playing at the center,
holding the earth to its natural spin,
mothers, daughters, and nieces, daughters-in-law,
conversed about the somewhat more believable,
but still mystical.

The horror of the farm couple
down the road
found bound hand and foot,
shot with their own shotgun.

A baby born missing an arm.
A family curse, star-crossed,
insanity skipping two generations,
the affliction of drink in husbands,
every woman's nemesis. And
practical wisdom, the advisability
of keeping doors locked
or taking Epsom salts and
Carter's Little Liver Pills for cramps.

It was a matter of wedding rings,
lunar cycles, the endless repetitions
of cake walks and birthdays,
of what was passed on circling back
as easy and natural to them as Plato's forms.

But something in what the women said,
the large Seth Thomas on the mantel
barely, but always audible above their cyclical voices,
there was something in what they said
that the men did not hear.

The women were saying you always come back
to where you are. And you bring yourself
back with you, and that's that. There's birth
and a time to sit down between that and death,
and no matter how many years apart,
all of it in the same room — and then
the world outside is not that different
from the inside, so it doesn't much matter
who rolled away the stone.

But the men were still talking about things
that lift off the average,
that might make a straight line run for open space,
even though it was mostly comforting to find them
settled again on earth, after all.

They were interested
in the strange blue light that lit up
the night sky of the entire northern hemisphere.
So moving the stone (although
it didn't much matter who moved it)
was only the beginning,
the first part of the improbability
of getting the door open
to get through to whatever is on the other side
that needs looking into.

BITTERSWEET

Mary Hutchman

At Thanksgiving we drive slowly along
the narrow winding gravel road
our annual family pilgrimage
to the ninth concession of Tyendinega:
an Irish Catholic settlement
once Mohawk territory.

We are oblivious of 'travel at your own risk' signs
as we search the roadside for bittersweet
tiny dots of orange, flowering
"in axillary or terminal clusters"
flowers unisexual, "sometimes perfect."
During autumnal ripeness, orange berries
split open, exposing orange red arils

We park the car, climb down into ditches,
thick with undergrowth
crawl up the other side,
stretch pussywillow-soft arms
through thorned branches,
tear off tangled reluctant woody vines,

heavy with ripe orange-red berries,
the centre, a brilliant true orange seed,
surrounded by a frilled red poisonous berry.
We fill the trunk full up, bicker
cover up our scratched flesh.

In spring we forget rubber boots
revel in sunshine and wet feet,
wade through ditch-filled water
to pick yellow cowslips, struggle
on into marshes to cut down long
strips of pussywillow, velvety soft,
run our fingers over silken pods
like Greek worry beads,
pick perfect white petalled trilliums,
try to ignore my brother who claims
to have been born under a lucky star,
that white trilliums are commonplace,
that only red trilliums and first born sons count.

PALOMINO PRAIRIE, RATTLESNAKE SUMMER
Bruce Hunter

With cousin Gary
skirting gravel shoulders of Crow's Nest Pass
under the fallen face of Turtle Mountain.

Boulders on the roadside
venerable as dinosaurs
looming over the CPR tracks and across the valley
that held a town until one morning in 1903.
Whether a miner's drill,
dynamite blast or last shout of bravado,
none of that matters.

A rotten slant of rock
waiting since Noah
slid over a town in its sleep.

Eyeing the mountain I step behind him
into the stone rubble:
a cellar, wooden chairs and a candle
inside the skull of a town
mystery dank on the walls.

Fingers pinching was from the flame
he tells me of uncle's palomino
pale sweetgrass with a sundog mane,
the hyperbole of memory.
Trucked north form the ranch at Pincher Creek
to run in the Calgary Stampede.
Driven into the rail before American tourists.
The rifle to its prize temple
where nothing is kept for beauty alone,
the utility of a bullet.

Later the uncured hide on the fence
flapping like frozen wash.
The chucked head in the gully, maggots frothy at the nostrils.
Everything in this country wind-toppled,
backed against the life.
The cable holding the barn against it,
the house leaning and uncle himself.

Homeward shushed along the highway
the colliery towns:
Frank, Bellevue, Blairmore.
Memorable bones, twisted carcasses of deer.
Stains on the road,
from the boulders they come to sun on the asphalt
being cold-blooded. Rattlesnakes, he shudders.

A road under, and around,

not a name but a nuance.
History, a mountain shouldering off centuries.
Two boys,
stone passed hand to hand.
A blade wedged in a post.
That skin spread before us
bloodied and sundried as a map
a cloud of rockdust, a shout.

WILDFLOWERS

Janice Kulyk Keefer

Passing us on the road
a farmer stops to ask *what ya want
with them ditch weeds down there?*
Spits, and hinders us from looking
till the dust his boots cloud up
eclipses him

and settles on these daisies,
sprung from gravel, soft heads furred
with summer dirt.

Blessed are the name givers.
Goldenrod and purple vetch,
chicory, wild carrot, fleabane,
viper's bugloss, horse-tail grass;

blessed these stiff stalks
and wily roots; the petals grudged
from rock and drought and dearth of eyes
to bloom and seed forever
over farmers' dry, ditched bones.

THIRST

Cornelia Hoogland

The earliest memory is licking
salt blocks set out in fields for cows.
Blue, indented where those long tongues rasped,
scooping saliva and salt.

I remember the tricks:
climbing with yellow boots on weathered boards,
balancing on the post long enough
to locate a speck of blue
acres away. Could've been sky.

I remember sun and running and
a blade released into wind
until there was nothing
recognizable.

Except those blue blocks
I'd lie beside,
risking a salty lick.

MIND OF HIS OWN

Kathleen Kemp Haynes

On a spring day, spread clearly behind the barn,
Moving across the stubbly field toward the line fence
I could see Dad and Big Tom joined by harness and plough,
Almost flying down the field, turning a black furrow.
Big Tom, not a farm horse at heart, but secret racehorse,
Never walked if he could run and never crossed a bridge.
The man who sold us this, our first horse, saw us coming,
Dad had to walk him through the creek, not down the lane,
Because our laneway crossed a rickety bridge.

Dad sprinted, steering the plough, while Tom pulled it, turn-
ing the furrow.
One-horse-drawn farmers didn't cultivate large tracts.
Big Tom was not with us many years; he wore out.
The tractor that took his place pulling a larger plough
Would take the bridge and larger machinery in stride,
And didn't shy at the sight and sound of gulls
That followed the plough even this far inland.
Of course, it never nuzzled softly for an apple
Or kicked up its heels out of the sheer joy of life.

UNTITLED

Phil Hall

A man walks through half of the sun
over fallow land toward warm windows
Each step he takes makes the earth boom
its guttural yodel in the air

Around him and outward in widening circles
animals scatter at breakneck and breakdown speed.
Their spasms of flight and of running
make the sould of hectic tin plinks.

In the warm house a woman is red on one side
brown as bread on the other as her thoughts strum
over the fireplace and the humming of children
over the vibrating blood of her husband's kill.

Near the garden the graves of their parents
lean together like a barbershop quartet
release their hopes in the lonely scraping of strings.

MILK AND HONEY

Jim Green

Not milk and honey
for all of them,
not by a long shot.
Out east of here
on the open prairie
forsaken homesteads
hidden in coulees
roofs slumped in
walls leaning
vacant window holes
door frames askew
and inside one
testimonial relic
desperate letters
scratched on wood

FROZE OUT
DRIED OUT
BLOWED OUT
STARVED OUT

FAMILY

Jim Green

All of us - my Mother, sister, two brothers and my Uncle used to sit around the table in the evening sorting wheat with our fingers laughing by the light of the kerosene lamp making sure we got all the buckwheat out talking about things that happened that day cleaning out the wild oats and mouse dirt

We had a hand grinder bolted to the cupboard and we'd take turns cranking the wheat Just once through to crack it for porridge three or four go-arounds for bread flour Somebody would put the kettle on for tea and for once we'd all put our elbows up smiling sleepily over our steaming cups

Our rough porridge took four hours to cook so Mother always precooked it each night Sometimes she'd bake bread in the evening and the cabin would swell with the glow first the dough with the sweet yeast rising then the warm bread fresh from the oven smeared with a swath of chokecherry jelly

One year we had no money to buy kerosene so we used a bowl of bear fat with a rag It gave off a flickering and smokey light but we'd sit around the table for homework or to play cards by the wavering flame All of us together around our own table a warm circle of family

STRUCK

Patrick Friesen

late afternoon sun blazes off birch trees and I'm caught by a
	clearing where I was born
I know that light like I know the wind that spoke and speaks
	light as linen on a line
I remember how the mind moved rustling like a small animal
	in underbrush skittering among the leaves

there is room for sadness here this is the place where a boy
	understands more than he knows
barbed wire and wild roses the tangle of a man's life how he
	encounters himself looking back
an old hand on the bark of a willow his eyes still wondering at
	the fish lurking in the creek

you know how it works how you have to stand still letting the
	light climb up your trunk
you have to forget most things human this is not a place where
	anything has happened
you are a man I don't know how else to say it you are a man
	who has always sought god

there is a kind of indifference here hushed and slow it doesn't
	matter when you go
it doesn't matter what you know you are always a child here
	neither lost nor found not making strange
there is nothing you owe but the words you come to and those
	words are your seal

there is room for a mind between the high prairie sky and this
	scrappy undergrowth
how the air stirs shifting from one silence to another something
	about to happen
bare thickets in the fall a last pale rain arriving the way distant
	thunder hollows out the afternoon

the boy learns to stand among the trees a kind of listening at
    the edge of things
it's the step in that kills the man released into the open helpless
    and abandoned
if it wasn't for the rain who could live through the clearing if it
    wasn't for that mercy

AFTER THE TORNADO

Tony Cosier

As soon as the storm has blown its breath out,
Families who huddled away come stumbling back.
Neighbours come with the morning light. And keep
On coming for miles around in widening circles,
County by county. Then even strangers arrive.

Flattened walls go up again.
Windows slip back with new glass in.
Clusters of carpenters nail shingles flat.

Fields are cleared. Fenceposts meet rails.
Splintered elms are cut and stacked.
A new barn lifts from an old barn's boards.

Yet those who have lived here for years will find one day
Not too far off where quiet will settle back
and fear will subside enough that a bit of a push
On the welltower's windmill pump will bring no fret
And hardly a memory, except perhaps the thought
Of a pivot in the human heart that pulls men together
When the going is tough and bolts them hard to the earth.

COME WINTER

Julie Berry

driving down to the farm something's changed the birds are
only birds now the sky behind them smudged someone with
dirty fingers reached for them and missed walking up the long
hill they fly around me but they don't talk to me why is that?
they've always called out before wherever i was risk every-
thing risk it risk it

when i get to the farm there are twenty or more old boxes
stacked up under the plum trees old banana boxes full of
receipts and cash register tapes rolled into neat bundles with
elastic bands you gotta keep them a certain number of years for
the income tax says grandpa and there's two big holes dug in
the back lawn grandma tells me the septic tank's not working
grandpa's dumping the pail way out back just like old times
she's not using the walker anymore though she's limping a lot
we go and sit in what used to be the parlour but now it's their
bedroom too i was just upstairs yesterday says grandma and
made it airtight but when i told your aunt vera you should've
heard her she says i can't go upstairs anymore i'll break my hip
all over again it doesn't feel right sleeping downstairs she
shakes her head i've slept upstairs all my life grandpa changes
the subject seems he's heard a rumour the government's going
to cut off the old age pension if they do that there'll be frozen
bodies all over the place come winter he says ya won't be able
to walk down the street without tripping over them thank god
i'll be dead soon he says
always knew it'd get this bad

EUCHRE PARTIES, FULLARTON TOWNSHIP

Barry Butson

Saturday evenings on the farm
of my only living grandmother -
hostess of wild hair.
Card tables set up on linoleum floor
of kitchen and wooden floor of living room
All the relatives—her sons and daughter,
their grown children and me,
only one still a child—are present,
despite the usual storm-warning.
We have driven in for euchre,
guaranteed laughter and certain
competition at cards. No booze, just
tea biscuits and pie washed
down with coffee, tea or milk.
All the short dark men
and women, her Irish brothers and sisters,
have gone white in the hair
and red in the face. They're the size
of elves, boots barely reaching the floor
as they prop their elbows on the tables
for a looksee at their hands, then glance
at partners for sign or signal.
So simple to cheat at euchre if you really wanted.

One game ends and they switch tables.
Someone keeps score, probably my grandmother,
so at the end before sliding off into snow
winners can be declared and a booby prize
awarded amid good-hearted snickers
and backslaps.

I was too young to play then,
but my own elbows
visited every table,

my eyes swept the four faces
of my elders as they gauged cards
and brazenly bid or cautiously
sat in the bush.
I felt the tables wobble
as my uncles and great-uncles slammed down every card,
as if forcefulness was the key to success.
(It <u>was</u> with their livestock).
I listened to those deep cattle-calling voices
yell out "euchre" so everyone in the house
could appreciate their opponents' humiliation.
It seemed natural that none of the women
would ever enter into this oneupsmanship.
If they won they were silent, if euchred
they giggled. It seemed natural
and it was not from them - at least for
a few decades - that I was learning.
I began to see
that life must require this
forceful display
of whatever you've got to offer,
that siffing in the bush may be productive,
but it was hardly what a fellow should do
on a regular basis.
Take a chance, trust your partner,
slam down those bowers...
that's what I was taught.

In the back seat on the way home,
though the car slipped and slid
underneath us, I slept.

I slept for a long, long time.

A THOUSAND DELICATE SAUCERS

Julie Berry

grandpa died in the tim horton's parking lot his cherry pie
half-eaten on the dash no doubt his spirit rose quickly and
when he looked down on his daughter and his wife as they
kneeled over his body he saw their hands like frightened birds
flutter over his heart crashing crashing into windows like a
cold starling heaven whistled down the chimney when grand-
pa died the air over our town swelled with music from the old
time gospel hour until the trestle over sunset trembled

from up there grandpa saw the old ford stir up years of dust
along the back concessions while he delivered the mail for
hazel and roy or sweet corn and strawberries to palmer's red
and white in shedden bush road coon road lake road scotch
stacey's jones's the root sisters goldie and emerson cryan from
up there the row of norway spruce receded the rogue springs
trickled down the lane into green jewelweed

he loved everything then the sand of the laneway the smell of
pineapple weed in summer the basin of warm water on the
back porch the cake of soap floating rows of tobacco picked
leaf by leaf tied onto slats hanging in the red insul-brick kiln
cured to gold

in the dark winter-shack under the pear tree he and grandma
bundled the velvet leaves into bales weighed them got them
ready for the auction 0 he did he did love everything then even
the horse that kicked him that set his tea quivering in a thou-
sand delicate saucers

PSALM FOR PROSPERITY

Michael J. Wilson

I wear caps advertising
the businesses of friends,
of fishtugs and trucks and pubs.
I wear their T-shirts, sweatshirts, jackets,
my working wardrobe halved by them.
I drive their roads and stroll their lands;
nourished on local produce
my girth orbits at peace.

We are the heirs of humbled hills,
even the weather is almost tame.
Think about it, we're shooting at planets
and sighting on stars,
never had it better
and there's no reason for better not to come.
For me, the sun is a patient horse,
and the earth, a bucket of oats.

I proclaim the glory of friends,
in logo, upon my brow, upon my breast.
I am an optimist of their optimism
celebrating casually a formal distinctiveness:
the surnames and the services,
the companies and the clubs.
They promote me by investiture in holy orders.
I bless them with my body.

STOUT

Barry Butson

Grown now into the shape
of my farmer father and uncles—
built for plowing
and tossing bales
so unpenlike,
such a waste to only write
poems and read books
with eyes born to see thunder
and arms made to climb haylofts.

Wider and wider
shorter and shorter I grow
squarelike over this desk
to circle my roots.

PROMISED LAND
(Alberta Dust Bowl, 1935)

Paul Benza

Everything is bitter here.
It is the taste of lies,
The taste of dust & sallow sky
Where wind always finds its way.
This is the land that will no longer feed us,
Deliver us the necessity of life.
This is wasteland.

There are no harvests here;
There are no seeds to sow, or
Rows to furrow & tend.
When the wind uses its knife

You can hear the ground begin to scream.
Armies of dust rise in barren fields
The way nightmares rise black into dreams.
Three years now, & our hones are tired,
Our bodies hollow with pain.
The graves of our ancestors are
Blown away like forgotten chaff.

Wind crucifies the future & rapes our past.
The sun is blind in the sky.
We have nothing left. Nothing.
In this season of Hell's own wind,
In this promised land
We once called home.

DROWNED LAND

Stan Dragland

I feel so lonesome facing the flood of 19—. That road is washed out—so much water on the prairie, the prairie so flat the water spreads and spreads. Lake Agassiz. You only learn later where you were. There is a sepia photo. A father in a rumpled suit—he has been driving in the suit. Why would he not at least remove his jacket in the heat? A suit and a fedora. The sweat from his brow has soiled the felt above the sweat band. Most of this is invisible in the photo. He stands, and his wife stands beside him, looking into the flood. There is a child in his arms and though that child is a girl with bobbed hair, she is also me, as I am also—thanks to my Ontario distance— this camera/man seeing and saying to you what I see. Having flown across the ocean to do so in Germany. And when I return to Canada it will not be to my second home in Ontario but to Newfoundland whose songs and stories and jokes travelled west and began to make a Newfoundland inside me.

But that couple — forlorn — with their forlorn child, they had
hoped for something new in these bad dry years. There was
news of land north of that now-uncrossable water where they
could homestead, land the government would give them just
for improving it. Now the future is drowned.

Say what you like. Say what the textbooks tell about Lake
Agassiz, how it covered the prairie after the ice age. Say any-
thing you want, it's still not right that so much hope should be
dashed in 19— by a flood that dried up millennia ago. Those
people had drifted for years like prairie topsoil in the wind,
and now they were going home to a land that had drowned. It
just isn't right.

THE SILENCE OF HORIZONS

Steven Michael Berzensky

"I liked New York.. But then, for me,
it grew horizontal — monotonous."
   —Jasper Johns, artist,
   Newsweek, Oct. 24, 1977

Here, on the prairie, day after day, this
horizon becomes the mute accomplice to history.

In one village (population: endangered),
near the only grain elevator, I am shown

a white house abandoned, its front window
crossed by planks. My friend gestures at it,

says the old man who lived there, a widower,
lost his mind, hanged himself inside. A passing

remark. Our soles scuff the gravel road. The green
screen door rattles behind us after we step
inside the general store for some family provisions.
(It is meagerly stocked.) Outside the store, he

shrugs toward the horizon: "Once a man does that
to himself, there is nothing more to say.

I take my time to look. The horizon glows red,
sputters out. The white house slowly darkens.

STONEBOAT

Joe Blades

Driving along secondary roads gravel roads back roads the
back forty   at this junction a tilted wagon wheel of rusted
mailboxes but no houses no farms in sight just ditches trees
the tiredness of fields that are no longer fields

There are signs of old fields still fenced   posts rotted off at
ground level   hanging together on rusted barb wire   a few
cows foraging between birch and spruce regrowth   forest
taking back the land   this stone and clay soil too difficult to
farm well

Here almost missed in the regrowth ruts ridged with grass
alders crowd a road in   foundation stones all that's left of a
farmhouse burnt   the hole criss-crossed with blackened beams
flowers and lilac bushes wax berry bushes rhubarb apple
trees gone unpruned and at least one ancient tree maple red
oak horse chestnut

Nearby collapsed outbuildings and spread wings of the barn
roof still peaked   wasp nests likely underside so don't go
crawling on top   hand-hewn beam walls fallen sideways
shingles weather-grey with pale green lichens some torn away
by wind or mossed over   hand-forged square nails sticking

out where the shingles are gone   underneath are barrel hoops
and sprawls of staves leg-hold traps for muskrat beaver and
bear horseshoes ox shoes and bells pitchforks peavey broad
axes crosscut saws smithy tools ploughs and harrows

We'll take it all home   make the basement the inside of a barn with
the beams remorticed   the grey weathered planks nailed hack on
hang a dart board between the rusted traps and tools put shelves
up for Zane Grey   Louis L'Amour and Max Brand Hammond
Innis Alistair MacLean Pierre Berton and Farley Mowat add
a tv stuffed squirrel (with lead sheet pipe-tray moulded into the
wood)   stuffed mink (hit be an Acadian bus out front of the
Bimsdale house)   stuffed silver-tipped fox (found killed by the
road)   add comfortable chairs a phone extension   there's room
for a woodstove the painting group will love it

Downfield in the swampy bit by the stream the farm dump:
rusted cans dish and crock shards Burdock's Blood Bitters bottles
liniment and druggist's bottles milk bottles clear beer bottles
blue black brown aquamarine and purple glass   wheel rims
mattresses coconut shells shoe leather rocks and more rocks

Bring the bottles home and any dishes you find they'll catch the after-
noon light brighten the basement windows get dusty like in the barn

More rocks than foundations and walls could ever want
stones pulled and prised from fields every year and beside the
stone pile sunk lower than low into the ground the stoneboat
grass and alders growing up through its punky planks   the
team of oxen brass belled pulling slow and steady dragged it
slow over fields waiting while small stones are tossed boulders
rolled onto the ground-level boat hauled it to the untillable
hollows the swampy bit by the creek to the dump   days and
days of rolling field stones on and then off   going back for
more and there are always more stones more back-breaking
work more stones than years of farming can hope to clear off
the fields every winter frost heaves and spring releases a new
crop more stones rising from the ground more stones to sink
under the weight of

WHAT'S LOST

Barry Butson

What is lost is the barn of my uncle
before milking, or the still-horned bull
and back corner of the far field.

What is lost is an aunt baking a pie;
it isn't there, never in my nostrils.
Grandparents hang by threads in attics,

maybe a hot buffered tea biscuit at best,
mainly just photos of farmers,
the women sitting in wicker on lawns

beside peony bushes, their husbands
standing behind in suspenders, moustaches
white as sugar on their plough-brown faces.

No sweating beside them stooking, no
heavy breakfasts in their back kitchens.
No sitting on porches at sundown

watching the dog bring home the cows.
I was last-born and doomed to miss
all this. Imagine Uncle Loril slurping

his tea from the saucer, as he preferred.
Looking up across the table at you,
with laughing eyes. Imagine the bush

behind those farms, its suburb of fox
and quail, streets of raccoon and dove,
woodpile of snake and wasp. Sugar shack

in December a destination worth heading for
with a Collie across frozen furrows and shallow snow,
opening the door to the warmth of mice and bat.

Sitting down like Zhivago at a rough table,
taking out a pen in gloves with fingertips clipped,
getting it down before it disappeared. Imagine

the crows outside calling.

WHAT LAND MEANS: AUTUMN 1998

Anne Compton

The Horse Chestnut dies from the bottom up
the leaf withers from the edge inward.
Until that explosive moment, your heart
kept its secret: No tatters on the summertime of your age.

Youngest sons aren't supposed to leave first.
Didn't you know that? Abandoning all.
Overtaking autumnal brothers and sisters, you fell
asleep on your feet, the quick stride stilled
between house and fields.

The last thing seen, they say, is forever held in memory.

So you could see those fields still (by times, coasted,
cultivated, cropped), we planted you
on the down slope of a hill: Advantage to all your acres,
a family loam richest in you, Great Tree. Hold me
in view. Wait at the bottom till I coast to you.
We'll climb up together. Into green branches.

CROSSING THE WINTER FIELDS

James Deahl

Slowly the vineyards emerge from early morning darkness;
last night's loose snow slants through them pushed by the
     white wind.
Dawn, and only the Mennonites are awake,
busy as wasps in winter's frozen heart.

Now orchards can be seen at the shore of the lake,
every knotted branch outlined by ice, by fresh pure snow.
After the Bible is read in the room of cold wood, the work
     starts
—always the work—numb hands patiently learning to love
     this land.

Matthew tells us we draw good from the store of goodness
     within our hearts;
and that evil is summoned form our stores of evil.
Fine grains of snow blow across the farmland.
Driven by my desire for forgiveness, I have come here.

Beside the frozen lake the dark body of a hawk plummets
     through cold air.

THE GRANGE

Tony Cosier

One pale spearhead in a tuft of green
Led to a second spear and the orange flare
Of a lily. We tugged the grass in handfuls
To open a mound of them and kept on going
To bare a wall of stones. We uncovered a log
Dense and thick as a west coast giant

And dug the earth in parallels in front and behind,
Chopping the sod and shaking the rich soil free.
We planted flags and coreopsis, daisies and columbine;
In the shade of the elderberry, bleeding heart
Then fern; and in the rougher places, shrubs.
We topped a bank with a golden flowing moss.

Bluebirds nested in the corner post.
Sparrows flicked in, with blackbirds in flocks.
Thistledown brought on hawkweed, clover, lace,
Mullein that coiled in a furry braid
To lift tight kernelled in a mammoth thrust
Towering above our heads with a thousand yellow tongues.

Behind the mound patrolled by guardian snakes
Where empty air was once a barn, tall grasses
Whisper across the foundation stones, urge
The mind to imagine ghostly walls come up again
To open at us doubledoored on giant
Squealing hinges, like a cornucopia
So rich and real the garden itself spills outward
As an overflowing harvest from the grange.

NUISANCE GROUNDS

Olga Costopoulos

The poison green combine, whose flaking paint
has survived its more solid metal parts,
hulks useless, monstrous on the skyline,
unable to settle into decent rot,
much less venerable entropy,
awkward in deserted limbo between
obsolescence and antiquity.

Our trash, unfit for a public landfill
gets hauled away to the pasture
where rust-red Herefords graze,
and sometimes maim themselves
on the snaggle teeth of old hayrakes
that have rusted to jagged treachery.

Wrought iron bedsteads — so many here
archeologists will suspect it
the midden of some ancient brothel.
Or perhaps surmise the truth:
inhabitants so lazy
they mostly wore out beds.
But five washing machines bear witness
to a clean establishment — of its kind.

I took away a brown glass gallon-jug
intact, it didn't seem to belong here,
a golden-amber pumpkin growing
on tangled frozen vines of rusting cable
whose only other fruits were half-crushed cans,
their only flowers discarded chrome hubcaps
tendrilled with loose wild bedsprings.

TURNHILL

T/Ed Dyck

In the saucered plain
where the ridges roll in the dust
and the hot sun crawls
over runted trees
there
stands the hill where the cattle turned.

Out of the smoky lovelies
along the gullies
where the land
plunges
wild as a pony to the river
he galloped away

Away from the lip
of the promised land
where the trees smouldered
at the foot of a turning hill
and the house went down
with a slap and a splash.

Still
the land hangs
as a hawk
hunting the river-breaks
and as a man-made tide washes
washes the hill where the cattle turned.

SAWTOOTH ROADS

Joe Blades

Up the mountain sawtooth
tractor roads   Forrest pipe smoking
drives   In the apple bin hooked on
the back of the tractor   among rotting
cabbage leaves for deer   Norm and I stand
He wears a chicken blood-stained smock and
hardhat from work at Cunard Poultry in Canning
The dog   who confuses me with Forrest's
son — a Mountie in Saskatchewan — jumps in and
out of the apple bin   barking
as we climb steep buldozered roads

Slowly we wend our way to the
top and Gloosecap's legendary home
We dream aloud of potential cabin sites
past and coming deer hunts   comment on
potato and apple pickers in fields
orchards now far below   take farm
photos plan the necessary
winter woodcuts

Here for only a few weeks of
work better than any lived 'til now
Why would I leave this life:
the bushels of fresh-picked apples
cliff mud on amethyst crystals
weekly church suppers   herding
milk cows   splitting firewood
Next week I go to Toronto   leaving
an incomplete harvest behind
Pieces of me left growing

WINTERING OUT

James Deahl

By Loon Lake
the fields lie flooded,
uncut corn stands
trapped in ice,
even the moon's
locked in its frozen sky.
Surrounded by orchards
farmhouses stand
heavy as iron
the whole night through.
Amid the bare trees
they are the bells of loneliness

wintering out the dark months,
waiting for spring
to strike them pure.

A FAR CRY

Lea Harper

It takes two days
Nemaska, then Chisasibi
Almost at the treeline
the landscape dwindles
to jack pine
Towns evaporate

No roads before the dams—
surging waters gagged and harnessed
Now stopped rapids—
boulders black and menacing
like a pile up of cars
and where 10,000 caribou drowned—
the methane of rotting vegetation
Miles of scrub and sky
a cold desert highway—
chinks in the Canadian Shield

At check point
the drummer taps his knees
The story of *Malcolm* slips off his lap
Son of a diplomat
a solitary black boy in Ottawa
his thoughts are impossible to read

We're unlikely tourists
They want ID
In history class I learned

my people were savages
The bass player nods. He's Cree

It's all a front the glossy brochures
They're tracking threats to the infrastructure —
the next White Whale Project

The land quakes under the weight
of man-made rivers
White fish, mercury-tainted
glow in the dark
Those who eat them feel the tremors

Startled by huskies with ice-blue eyes
at rest stops he sticks with *Malcolm*
his own canteen and dwindling supplies
In Pretoria I walked on the hoods of cars
to escape the dogs
Night falls under the grit of stars
a cloud of gravel
We are like a lost migration of geese
over James Bay
Most of us died on merchant ships
packed together like sardines

Malcolm slips off the map
X marks the spot, a thousand miles
from nowhere

At journey's end
there are cook tents waiting —
bannock, berries and moose
a bonfire, honour drum
fiddles, step dancing

First black they've seen
except on TV
Children touch his woolly hair

He is something wild and rare
like the random appearance
of a wolf or bear
He has never been made to feel
this welcome

It's a far cry from Africa
further still from the Capital—
this part of Canada
he never knew existed

WHY THE FIELDS LIE FALLOW

Bruce Hunter

True, there will be the usual crops:
corn, gourds, and blossoms in the orchard.

But the man is gone.
His wife remains in the new house
at the end of the orchard, the retirement home.

She watches the new couple
who bought the fields, the barn
and everything that came with them
the house where her children were born.

She sees in them all the photographs of the past.
She will find herself walking,
never in time quite reaching them.

She will reach out and touch what is real,
the cold heads of cabbages,
snapping fingers of beans.

121

Birds trail the harrow
as they have always done
and with mechanical twists make worms disappear
from the furrows of tawny earth.

Later she will sort their possessions
and pile them in a pyre on the hillside
where they used to burn the prunings
from the orchard, her and her other.

When the wind bangs the door on its hinges at noon,
she will catch herself
turning in that familiar way.

For a time her daughters will come home weekends,
take her hands in those moments
when she no longer remembers she is strong.
That it was her he looked to.

But soon she is alone again
with the silence, only the sounds of the apple boughs
rapping on the house.

At dusk the dog will follow her
to the hillside under the black walnut tree
near the son who could have taken this from her.
She will remember how they buried him
and later all the children's pets,
the ceremony and the small crosses
overlooking the grassy slopes
that roll down to the river.

One day she will return
one furrow, wider and darker, open before her.
The arms of her husband and her children
will beckon her.

PICTURE PERFECT

David Hillen

A small, southwestern, Ontario farm
      nestled
      near a bend in the road
      a small creek
      and the necessary bridge:

midst the May-green grass
on these fields of peace
three mares and three colts:

Big is beautiful.
Small is beautiful.
Roan is beautiful.
Alive is beautiful
— is everything.

IN ALL THE CHURCHES

Bruce Hunter

small towns and rivers without water
in a land marked yellow for dry miles
fenced with poles cracking grey, wires strung
with the black bead of cowbirds mocking
men tearing at the land significant in time
as the blackbird but ragged ash in somber wind
for the mother tongue of flame forewarns:
there will be no green this year

dragoned tongues toss black chaff
into the milling winds
barns and cattle disappear

while the county's crew watch
from the empty pumper
flame spills wire
from the burnt black stubs of poles
stealing light from the day
dust fools streetlamps into an early evening
fire is front page news
rain is prayer in all the churches

MOTHER AND DAUGHTER

Laurence Hutchman

What do I remember about Emery?
That was nearly forty years ago.
Yeah, we had good times.
There was always work to be done:
cutting the corn, mowing the hay, milking the cows...
you did that without complaining.
No, I got nothing more to say about Emery
"Hurry up nurse, and finish my manicure."

Why would someone want to write about Emery?
I spent my life trying to forget the place.
That's all I have to say.
Why does a stranger call me up
dredging up the past.
My stepparents couldn't even bother
to show up for my wedding,
had to go to the Saturday market.
I would have done anything to get off that farm.
Never knew much good there anyway
except for the neighbour who I fell in love with,
left my husband and children for.
My chemotherapy starts Thursday,
and on the weekend my daughter will be here
asking questions about our relationship,
    oh, won't these fingernails ever dry.

BLACK CREEK PIONEER VILLAGE

Laurence Hutchman

I linger under the loft in the alcove,
look through the panes of the frosted window
at a Christmas in York in 1840, imagine the wind
outside the farmhouse, blowing in expectation.
I see a girl with ruffled petticoats holding her porcelain doll,
a boy in Victorian clothes kneeling over his steel toy train.
"Time to move on, students," says Mr. Calvin.
We climb onto the horse-drawn hay wagon,
lumbering across the dusty road of Steeles.

In Joseph Stong's big barn
I touch barley rakes, pitchforks,
feel gritty wooden surfaces of butter churns.
I stand in the wide doorway,
a cold wind blowing around us
as the old man talks about threshing,
"This was the way we separated wheat from chaff."
I lift up the fallen wheat,
letting it trickle in streams of golden grain;
the dusty chaff blows away, a parable of Judgement Day.

I am walking here, always walking and thinking ,
trying to place myself a hundred years ago,
(harvesting the fields before the coming of winter)
cracking a secret joke with George and Steve
still feeling the grain in my palm.
I clamber up the hillside,
pause before a garden: the spices of the world.
Here leaning on the fence in this November twilight
I inhale rich scents slowly, pronounce under my breath:
tarragon, thyme, sage, coriander
—names of the never-to-be-forgotten girls
Carla, Gloria, Louise...

LET ME DESCRIBE IT

Carole Glasser Langille

Let me describe it. Don't glance back
  at the farmhouse. Uphill, inside
a decrepit fence, cows, some goats
  a horse. Then nothing but scrub
till the road curves. Turn right.
  What is it about this stretch of woods
that's so otherworldly? In ten minutes
  you can traverse the length. But once inside
massive spruce and pine, pulled from roots,
  sprawl over paths. Light from a barely visible sky
dazzles moss, that plush, velvety cushion
  so dense it seems
not to carpet but to roof us
  with its light.
Something wild lives here,
  and when I wander, though briefly,
I feel a slight unease. Will a tree fall,
  some animal plunge? Still,
I hate to leave. But how stay?
  ...This need to be private, solitary. Yet
to reveal as well. Not to keep secrets,
  perhaps because of, not despite, the solitary.
Returning to town I walk by the ocean,
  past seaweed left on shore: a tart acidy green
almost too pungent to look at.

THE 401 TOWARDS MONTREAL

rob mclennan

the country a landscape like a wound, opens
& closes w/ each generation history weeps
         & eroding stars curve down
            their sharp edges. the earth,
itself,

begins to forget. a few fields away
    from the ruined church, newly
         locked from learning hands, sab-
rina
     barefoot thru the long grass

     & leaking pot smoke, a pilfer
       from her mothers drawer,
three years before she disappeared,

     w/out as much as a mention or a new address.
     a west wing bangs barn doors, shutters.
         *

     a good place to be, they say.
     a good place to be from. even so.
where the old highway 2 still follows, a lake
a line at lancaster & the american bridge
       hanging over the heavens from corn-
wall.
a wall of growing corn.

where friends still live & die, new
houses built on parents land, & continuing

    the family tree, a business
older than I am, you.

where were you when you were here, how
close. two old poets & one wife
in transcanada driving montreal
        to toronto line

when I was barely big enough
to do the two-step, thru old
glengarry. angela hallucinating visions
    on the sides of barns, where
once they stoppt. & do they
                still remember,
        & think.

COUNTRY WALK

Robyn Sarah

Two who pause
at a bend in the dirt road
to read the names on stones
in a tiny plot—the names
on four stones in a row,
a four-stone, family plot
(white-graveled, starkly graced
with plastic flowers in a gilded pot)

Two who stand
and ponder the bare dates
and the tale they tell
(how two, called only
Daughter and Son, nearly
a century ago, survived
in turn, a mere three years:
the plain small headstones
square-edged, freshly cut,
recently placed
beside the parent stones
—replacing makeshift markers?)

Two who turn
to leave (finding
the way back not so long
as the way there, for being
familiar now)
move closer to each other
in their walking, and touch hands,

while at their backs a wild rose wind,
chasing the road dust, hurries them home.

SUMMER FALLOWING

William Robertson

Used to bad years
they don't spend in the good
only the words
from only the designated few
storytellers for the town
words flowing like water
that never fell
bad land, bad luck
good men, strong women
spending it all in one night
then back tomorrow
turning, turning again
keeping weeds from the fallow.

ABANDONED FARMHOUSES, REPRISE

Brent Robillard

Did I speak to you
of ghosts?
The Pale Ones
who peep
through cracked
and broken panes
and warm their hands
by empty stoves
in kitchens
so long out of use
even the walls
have lost
their Sunday-dinner scent?

It is they
who teach the house
its sadness,
mope through rooms
as quiet as the moon
and scatter dust
in motes of light.
It is they
who cause the floors to snap
and walls to moan
like frightened children
in the night.

But they are not at home here.

Like in-laws,
they were just passing through
and never left.
Like me,
they found the place abandoned.

The only difference is, to them,
it was worth more than just a poem,
more than death.

DREAM: JUNE 1998—TOTEMS

for Marshfield Woods, destroyed January, 2000

Laurie Smith

a gravel road
between essex and kingsville
country, farm, desolate...
somewhere past a house with
spruce windwall to the north
a rust angora rabbit—I

picked it up and
it turned white, wanted to go alone
as I tried to carry it away

then I was in a clearing on the west
side of the road
cloistered by
beautiful naked coniferous
tall burnt pines and fir,
saw small totems carved up bodies
then entire ghostly faces, whispering
Iroquois, Iroquois
towering over me
like titans

in the corner was a dry pond covered
with broken trunks, arms, legs
arranged photographically, the decomposing
spines of antiquity
dark browns and greys and silver silence
I dropped in supplication or instinctual fear
and veneration for this place

the wind above me rattled like a snake,
the branches—dream was trembling, quaking
at my feet but faster, faster, running
thunder roll then quiet

and in the utter stillness, all as one
the wall of trees began to wave and shudder
backwards, leaned away
to fall on clamor
saws and bulldozers, plows

I saw the county's tools beat in a path
across the solemn glen
and coward, urban coward,
ran awake

LOCAL LANDSCAPE

Laurie Smith

macdonald, jackson, carr
celebrate the great canadianness of landscape;
we wonder if there is a landscape left in essex county.
we have our own jokes and complaints,
cut off the navel of london, excluded from canada,
fearful of the other country's city at our feet, our heads,
confused by our own geography.

we immerse in steel and blue plate glass river scenes,
concrete coffins, ribbons too high to see anything but sky,
trees parked at convenient intersections, all greying, thinning
to outskirts and bedroom towns among the corn and flat
beans,
seasonal oddities like strawberry speckled fields or waves of
sunflowers, wheats and pampas grass bulrushes
and purple loosestrife all higher levels of flat,

the semicircles merge onto 401 and away,
looking for,   looking for,
driving for another topography, driving for
hours to be impressed
by a mere roll of the highway, an event to your vehicle
that's never needed to test its emergency brakes
on a downhill grade, lessons skipped in local driving classes,
useful only in halifax or kamloops;

in principle, we know that walking is difficult elsewhere;
yonge street to rainy river would be the ultimate hike,
the glacial rubble of superior a challenge,
(we have no rubble of our own, only the occasional gravel spill
around new construction, crunchy refrozen brown slush,
stony snow parking-lot-scrapings/toboggan hills,
march potholes cratering the ways out of town.)

ONE WINDSOR DAWNING

Sandra Muse

Morning Crispness of new snow
shaken upon the front lawn
mask bumpy lumps of earth
and lonely forgotten leaves
Scattered birdfoot tattoos
etched upon white snowskin
nature's design of whimsy
man cannot hope to match.

ON THE WAY TO ZION AREA

John Tyndall

A drive on King's highways
county roads and concessions
through a new Spring season
feels like flying through heaven
on the way to Zion Area.

Red and white trilliums
bloom in wood lots
beneath buds of tree leaves
all the birches, poplars, maples
now softer elemental shapes
and away alone a last
rock elm still holds sway
in a certain field near Zion Area.

Farm acres lie fallow
grey corn stalks row on row
soil newly turned over
calls forth hungry seagull flocks
earth enfolds pungent manure
for miles around Zion Area.

Melted snows meet thunder-rains
and linger in low-lying corners
cattails twitch above marsh marigolds
new bulrushes sleep in dreams
just below the water's surface
in wetlands about Zion Area.

Whistling redwing blackbirds
flash come-hither shoulders
multi-hued kestrels scan
for mice or moles or voles
tree swallows and barn swallows
swoop   return   swoop   return
to the wires running to Zion Area.

Black vultures circle above
black crows strut below
for their torn carcass cuisine
ring-tailed raccoons
reawakened ground hogs
skinny barn cats and kittens
on the roads to Zion Area.

Wrought iron encloses cemeteries
pickets yield to barbed wire
electric fences next to cedar rails
demarcate horse stables, dairy barns
the wealthy spreads, the poorer farms
scattered around Zion Area.

With its own ancient graveyard
modest Zion Methodist
now Zion United Church
still opens its doors, its arms
to farmers, friends, families
but there are no fences
between the farms of Zion Area

only fenceposts.

ASPENS AFTER RAIN

Glen Sorestad

Only your feet remember
the soft sinking, one by one
into the springiness of autumn
carpet, only your nostrils
recall the flaring of senses
turning memory upsidedown,
or perhaps it's rightsideup.
The tramp of your feet
stir the aromatics of forest floor
where living and dead mingle
as old friends, where hidden fungi
wait to burst from shallow bunkers,
pale missiles of redolent darkness,
while the aspens quake
a creaky chorus and shed
their colours like aging strippers.

COMMON INTERCOURSE

Jane Southwell Munro

A long freight train drawn across the prairie
like a tape marked *Pull Here* on a box
of laundry soap. Green cattle cars, brown flat cars,
silver tankers: a sentence moving
its burden elsewhere. Word after word,
used over and over. Transports tying
the country together as love does a marriage.
The exotic quality of a whistle evoking longing
the way spreading a lather of suds
down your arms in the shower and watching
a spray of water undress you to the skin again
arouses an echo of early days
when buttons were for undoing. The way you longed
to speak French after a trip
to Percé. Riding a little train across the Gaspé
you saw the backyards of villages.
A woman hanging out her wash waved to you
and a man in a pickup stopped behind
a dropped crossing gate got out of his cab
and nodded at cars rolling by in a cacophony
of squealing wheels. You began to build another
vocabulary, laying down ties week after week,
but you never got far enough to ride its rails.
Now the desire for another
language relinquished, though the freight
rumbling east pulls your eyes along its line.
The weight of hard labour thunders through
a syntax vision. Could you begin again?

COUNTRY MATTERS

Penn Kemp

Via Rail, en route home from a weekend in London.
The man, arms up to put a valise in the rack,
cautions his son as the kids and I lug bags by.
A man not seen for half my life, but he knows me.
We visit, kids in one section, he and I in Smoking.

The photos I saw of us by coincidence yesterday,
flickering young faces settling before my eyes.
I never now how to respond to the immediacy of
the mirrors that surround us. Memories, he

presents an image of us together, how he saw us,
how we would have been. Not among my probable
futures even then. Smoke clouds them now.
I do remember he thought I had no style, he a man
of many styles he put on according to the weather.

"Do not let yourself be civilized," he says, "You
are the landscape." I lean against the window
seeing reflections of fields in my eyes, watching
a mind I am familiar with, that cave of blind end
subtleties burnished smooth by sea water. Words
rise and fall. I attend their resonance with care.

Small towns rush us by, wide open yards, kids
waving, Woodstock, fields again, flush with winter
wheat. Look for the hawk
                    on the dead elm.

"I did my dissertation on the pastoral because of
you. You were always in landscape and you keep
that part of you alive." We approach limestone
escarpment meandering rivers in grey flood.
Paris, Dundas. Winter's erosion baring the cliffs.

Burlington, Oakville. Softly, so I strain to hear:
"And I would still like to rape your guts out."

Car lots, the glint of sun on corroding metal on
asphalt. Tail pilings. Junk heaps of appliances.

"Look at this land. You already have." I leave
to be with the children for the last leg to Toronto

Union. Rear of the car please. Mind your step.

HOME

Carole Glasser Langille

I like returning.
Though something far ahead
pulls me. You know the joke:
If you don't know where you're going
any road will get you there.
Once my ex-husband said, "If you're lost
you haven't gone far enough."
Now, I rarely turn back.
Though once, confusing directions,
I went through a wood and came upon
what I thought was a field billowed with drifts.
Later I learned what I walked across
was the back harbour, frozen, covered with snow.
The unknown is always
drawing me closer. Always
it has held my weight, has never
let go beneath me.
On clear days I'm aware that what lies ahead
accumulates, grain by grain, in what's here.
At home, I'm determined to repair walls,
though cracks are codes worth deciphering.

I've been given trust because
no matter what I do with it, I believe
it's the key to this house I was meant to live in,
a house from which I can travel.

SONG

Colleen Thibaudeau

Tired old Ontario
landscape, you've got into my blood:

my heart is battersoft
as the last field pumpkin;
snake fences and steel spires,
you've brought me down

and

sometimes along the 401
I hear in the ancestors' keening
(that's the wind in the last elm)...

and

sometimes on CNCPVIA
all runs frenzied,
picking a line over
what's really the burning coals of Troy.

IF I GO UP THIS OLD ROAD AGAIN

Joan Finnigan

If I go up this old road again
into the country of my allegiance
drift into the silver village,
I can still hear on the summer Sunday porch
their mythomaniacal chuckles,
born of their nesting together
on Back Street behind the funeral home

From the broad Protestant-superimposed silences
of those clan sabbaticals
their laughter destined to echo
through the corridors
of my vibrant varicoloured life,
indelibly Celtic-Canadian,
poet at the right hand of kings

McCaras and McColgans,
two thousand miles of tears
out of County Cork,
to find a watery route
as ferry boatmen
across the tribalized river,
part of our journey as passengers
on moving bridges,
going home again

Up and down every road
cousins on every side;
on every village street
ancestral monuments,
towering verandahed bricks
my grandfather, "the man
who died laughing"
built as Master Carpenter
(can anyone in the alienated cities

understand what that means
to a sense of pride in belonging
to the ongoing pursuit
of genetic soul?)

All the timber baron's sons
from velvet village mansions
went off to the war
and became decorated war heroes,
so Haddley Hodgins hung himself
because he couldn't leave the family farm
and join up with the other lads

How long does it take
in a new country
to grow a legend?

And right by the little red schoolhouse
on the fringes of the village
a field of burgeoning mythology lies
beginning a hundred years ago
when Hogan, original settler
of the country called Canada,
performed original sin
on the milk-house floor,
cool as a cucumber,
with the hired girl,
nobody's child from a bad farm
back of Boyneville,
then borrowed from a cousin,
the blacksmith on Back Street,
to pay for an abortion
in Lower Town, Montreal.

Nobody's child came back alive
but how to repay the debt
without his wife knowing all?
the blacksmith was patient

but finally confiscated
Hogan's field
by the little red schoolhouse,
and then everybody knew it all.

How long does it take
to grow a legend,
create a mythology,
especially in a country
with no regard
for its history?
no defenses
for its cultural identity?

If I go up this old road again
into the country of my allegiance,
into the landscape of the silver village
can I still hear on the summer Sunday porch
their mythomaniacal conspiracies
born of their nesting together
on Back Street behind the funeral home?

Crossing over the tribalized river
on McCara and McColgan's moving bridge
I weep for my country
and all its betrayers,
witting and unwitting,
who build the new roads
that let the enemy in

Soon our children will be run down road-kill
just crossing over
for water.

IF SILENCE IS THE LOUDEST SOUND

Michael J. Wilson

An industrious man
steps out for coffee;
gonna take a couple of mornings off
to chat in company
of a strong work ethic,
proud of his mastery over land.
But this is only a related event,
for now, he is not here.
His machines are parked at the barn.

Why does it seem in back-country
that I am the only
doesn't ride a machine?

The weekenders are nearby,
the muck-rakers, getting a kick outa noise,
gearing up down round and round.

I'd rather not so much as leave tracks,
stepping and stopping between peepings,
leaping shadows and flicking tails;
across torn trails
I make for the leaves.

Why, by golly look at this!
Far as the eye can see,
a stream has been ditched
and straightened...
guess this ain't a spot anymore
for ten thousand years of song.

The land'll dry quickly now
and stay that way.

     Bye, so long, good luck,

frogs snakes turtles shrews
moles weasels kingfishers
snails clams darters hawks
fox rabbits grouse warblers
wrens finches snipe mantises
butterflies, and poets,

but there never were many poets,
maybe only one.
And I'm just now getting over grief
of another hidden meadow
bulldozed for corn...
it's gotta be ten years since
those owls left.

Such abrupt, strict, stunning stillness
compels an obsession keening
for the faintest note, for evidence,
for some echo amplified by absence.

Were we the last generation of children
to have played with fox snakes,
chased and poked a wood turtle for a day,
or loaded a bucket of salamanders,
or let a crayfish pinch a thumb,
or stalked a tree-frog among fireflies?

Mink hunted muskrat
and a cat could snack
from a very inclusive menu.

Accompanied by eagles and deer
where set the fences?
How is anything sacred?
and how is it not?
How loose, how bind?

Not a cloud in the sky...
up is a long way off
above blighted elms which allow
just the right dosage of ants
for woodpeckers one could come to know.

Perhaps, somewhat zennish, I'll let
None-Greater-Than-Can-Be-Thought,
the Great Spirit,
the Everywhere-and-All-at-Once,
do the talking, the pointing,
when suddenly
here It Is thanking me, saying
I am the pearl of great price
the land was purchased for...

In an oxbow grove
beech trees were engraved,
time and time again,
by horse riders picnicking,
carving hearts and arrows:

Derek Loves Jane   1973
Mandy & Bart   '58 fading...
like tracks
            in melting snow

ABOUT NOON
Colleen Thibaudeau

About noon
when the whistles blew with a cockscrow I came
out of the grey granary of the employment building
    onto Spadina,
at that point wide as a barnyard.

Truckers were unloading chickens in crates,
      redeyed scrofular
chickens much as children there with their beaks agape
to know they would be sold with fishes out of
      clearwater tubs,
hard naked as stevedore loaves and warty old vegetables.

The february sun shone typically toronto
        in a trickily gutter,
made a ray in my eyes like murine, all straw
coloured was the widewayed city then and a barnyard.
Over the bakery leaned a woman with a broadshawled bosom
        letting her son's name fall
from the windowsill. He came then
        applecheeked, coalheaded,
rushing along with his shoulders bang and check
(see he'll grow up a character from Aucassin)
        a puddle jumper and his blue
        zipper jacket rushing too;
There was a downflash of a dime for bread.
I thought this was the real colour of the land —
and had a Golden Goose flown over Kensington Market
with an egg for every pousey pocket,
        they were that gay.
I saw the overall factory workers through their cellar window
        drink a bucket of coke
        heard a joke in a strange tongue;
This was the real Canadian farm atmosphere of the golden age
the bee, the threshing where no methodist had been...

There was the engine roar of the team overhead on the barnfloor

they were drawing in

while we sailed shingles on the cold green horsetrough

and were children then

and as innocent of the power of horses that's a city's harnessed

power

as of that point where the quick quiet sight of sun on water

starts to make this poem

THERE

Derk Wynand

On the palm, blisters sing
the same old songs, old favourites
those hot rhythms again.

HAIKU

Marianne Bluger

'for sale'
& wind
in the empty barn

WHAT ONCE WERE FARMS
WILL SOON BE CITIES

Roger Bell

Seen them gathering
gulls, like circling farmers' ghosts
O, bereft, bereft
they cry to heedless dull machines
eating the dusty land

FARMHOUSES
Robert Sward

Climbing down from my tree, I visit my wife,
breakfast with her, read manuscripts and shave.
I walk out of the house into a ringing
like the ringing in my ears. It is the day —
sunlight, pine trees, abandoned farmhouses.
I have walked again into the landscape:
change of directions, turnings of the mind.

ACKNOWLEDGMENTS

Berry, Julie: "Come Winter" appeared in Canadian Forum, October 1995. "Poor Man's Pine" from Worn Thresholds, (Brick Books, 1995). Reprinted by permission of the author.

Blades, Joe: "Stoneboat" appeared in The Amethyst Review. Reprinted by permission of the author.

Bluger, Marianne: "Tanka" appeared in Gusts, (Penumbra, 1999). "Haiku" appeared in Tamarack and Clearcut, (Carleton University Press, 1997). "The Snowscape Puzzle" appeared in Nights Like This, (Brick Books, 1984). Reprinted by permission of the author.

Butcher, Grace: "Survival," and "The Old Farm Woman," appeared in Before I Go Out on the Road, (Cleveland State University Poetry Center, 1979/1992). Reprinted by permission of the author.

Clark, John Livingston: poems from Stream Under Flight, (Thistledown, 1999). Reprinted by permission of the author.

Costopoulos, Olga: poem appeared in Muskox & Goat Songs, (Ekstasis Editions, 1998). Reprinted by permission of the author.

Dyck, T/Ed: "Turnhill," appeared in Number One Northern Poetry. Reprinted by permission of the author.

Hunter, Bruce: "In All the Churches," appeared in Benchmark, (Thistledown, 1982). The other two poems appeared in The Beekeeper's Daughter, (Thistledown, 1986). Reprinted by permission of the author.

Kemp, Penn: "Etymology of Progress," and "Country Matters," appeared in Travelling Light. Reprinted by permission of the author.

Sarah, Robyn: "The Children on the Road," appeared in Questions About the Stars, (Brick Books, 1998). Reprinted by permission of the author.

Thibaudeau, Colleen: "About Noon," appeared in The Artemesia Book: Poems New and Selected, (Brick Books, 1991). "Song," appeared in The Patricia Album, (Moonstone, 1992). Reprinted by permission of the author.

MEMBRE DU GROUPE SCABRINI

Québec, Canada
2000